Books by B.J. Reinhard

Sanji's Seed

Glow-in-the-Dark Fish

Our Place in Space

Our Place in Space

B. J. Reinhard

BETHANY
BACKYARD®

www.bethanyhouse.com

Our Place in Space and 59 More Ways to See God Through His Creation
Copyright © 2001
B.J. Reinhard

Design by Lookout Design Group, Inc.
Cover and text illustrations by Greg Cross

Published by Bethany House Publishers
A Ministry of Bethany Fellowship, International
11400 Hampshire Avenue South
Bloomington, Minnesota 55438
www.bethanyhouse.com

Printed in the United States of America

Library of Congress Cataloging-in-Publication Data
Reinhard, B. J.
   Our place in space and 59 more ways to see God through his creation / by B. J. Reinhard.
     p. cm.
Summary: Sixty readings introduce the physical sciences and the wonder of God, covering such topics as the formation of clouds, magnetism, and electricity and including devotional thoughts, Scripture verses, and activities.
   ISBN 0-7642-2263-5
   1. Creation--Juvenile literature. 2. Physical sciences--Religious aspects--Christianity--Juvenile literature. 3. Children--Prayer-books and devotions--English. [1. Creation. 2. Physical sciences--Religious aspects--Christianity. 3. Prayer books and devotions.] I. Title: Our place in space and fifty-nine more ways to see God through his creation. II. Title.
   BT695.5 .R4425 2001
   261.5'5--dc21   2001002351

For Josh,
who also delights in seeing
God through His creation

About the Author

B. J. Reinhard's love for writing and nature began when she was a teenager in Colorado. She still lives in Colorado, where she enjoys the company of her husband, their two sons, a spunky yellow lab, multitudinous African violets, a desert rosy boa, and a pet carniverous plant.

Table of Contents

INTRODUCTION

Have you ever been surprised by the stars?

Several years ago I was. I remember driving deep into the Colorado mountains, far away from city lights. Climbing out of the car and into the silence of night, I looked up. That's when I experienced "the surprise." Above was a sky crowded with glittering stars. In some places the stars were so thick they stretched across the heavens in a filmy white band.

If you're a city dweller, then perhaps you've also been treated to "the surprise" when you've escaped the glow of man-made lights. Even if you live where man-made lights don't pale the night, the beauty of a sky packed with stars never fades, does it? Today when I travel away from the city, I'm just as surprised by the stars as I was the very first time.

There are many such delightful surprises in our world. The more we unmask the mysteries surrounding everything from atoms to rainbows to grains of sand, the more amazing our world becomes.

As much as these astonish us, though, the biggest surprises can come from discovering the God who put our world together. Learning that our vast universe holds a countless number of stars can make you feel small and unimportant. But learning that the God who knows the name of every single star also knows your name and cares deeply about you gives you a whole new way of looking at God and your life.

That's why *Our Place in Space* was written. I hope your sense of wonder and understanding about our physical world grows. Even more, I hope your sense of wonder and understanding of God grows so that your eyes will be opened to His greatness and love for you.

Our Place in Space features sixty chapters, each describing something from the world of science that relates to a theme about God and your life. A Bible verse and **Thought to remember** are included to encourage you.

The Bible verses listed are also meant to encourage you. At first it may seem easiest to just skip over them. But you might be surprised by what God can reveal to you through them!

Words that might stretch your **vocabulary** are in bold type. You can learn what they mean and how to say them if you jump over to the margin—just like it's shown here.

For hands-on fun that builds on the topic in each reading, check out the activities. You

vocabulary:
(vo-CAB-you-
LaRe-ee)
the group of
words you
know and use

may need your parents' help with some of them. Answers to puzzle activities are at the back of the book, starting on page 149.

If you'd like to explore more about any topic, **Dig Deeper!** lists key words and phrases you can use in a library or Internet search.

As you turn the page to begin *Our Place in Space*, think of yourself as beginning an adventure—an adventure to discover the breathtaking surprises found in our world and God.

① Atoms, Atoms Everywhere

Take a look around. What do you see?

Perhaps your world includes desks and donuts, walls and windows, kittens and clouds.

What are these made of? All sorts of substances! Wood, paint, plaster, flour, fur, and water are only a few. But what are *these* substances made of?

Atoms. These tiny, tiny particles are at the base of every bit of **matter** in our universe. You're made of atoms. So is everything else, everything from a fly's red eye to the stars in the sky.

Scientists have discovered that ninety different atoms exist in nature. More have been produced in laboratories. Some substances are formed of only one kind of atom. Silver, gold, iron, calcium, and oxygen are just a few you might know about. But most substances are formed when different kinds of atoms join together. That's how fewer than one hundred types of atoms can make the huge variety of materials in our universe. You might be surprised to find out that when you drink water, you're drinking one oxygen and two hydrogen atoms that are joined together. That's why we call it "H-2-O," which is written H_2O. It's interesting that oxygen and hydrogen are completely different when they're joined together than when they're apart!

For a long time scientists thought atoms were the tiniest building blocks of our universe. That was before they discovered the world *inside* the atom and learned that atoms are made of smaller building blocks. At the very center of an atom is a **nucleus**. It's packed with **protons** and **neutrons**. Whirling around outside the nucleus are **electrons**.

Now scientists know that even tinier particles make up protons and neutrons. In fact, protons and neutrons—and hundreds of other subatomic particles—are made from sixteen very tiny building blocks. But stay tuned! New discoveries are expected!

Amazing atoms are the basis for all matter in the universe. That's why you'll

matter: another word for substances; anything that takes up space and has weight

What atoms are you made of? Mostly carbon, hydrogen, oxygen, and nitrogen.

When two or more atoms join together they form molecules (MAH-lih-kyulz).

nucleus: (NEW-klee-us)

proton: (PRO-t'on)

neutron: (NEW-tron)

electron: (ee-ZEK-tron)

What about electrons? Are they made of tinier particles, too? Electrons are considered one of the sixteen basic building blocks.

> If I go up to the heavens, you are there. If I lie down in the deepest parts of the earth, you are also there. Suppose I were to rise with the sun in the east and then cross over to the west where it sinks into the ocean. Your hand would always be there to guide me. Your right hand would still be holding me close.
>
> PSALM 139:8–10

Have you ever heard that opposites attract? It's the reason atoms can join together. Protons have a positive electrical charge, electrons have a negative charge, and neutrons don't have any charge at all. The positive and negative charges of protons and electrons attract each other. And since an atom usually has the same number of protons and electrons, their charges balance each other out.

FIND IT!

Substances made up of only one kind of atom are called **elements** (EL-uh-ments). Below is a list of elements common in our lives. Find their names in the puzzle below. Names can be found forward, backward, up, down, and diagonally.

ALUMINUM	HYDROGEN	OXYGEN
ARGON	IODINE	PLATINUM
BORON	IRON	SILVER
CALCIUM	LEAD	SODIUM
CARBON	MERCURY	SULFUR
CHLORINE	NEON	TIN
COPPER	NICKEL	TITANIUM
GOLD	NITROGEN	ZINC
HELIUM		

```
B P L E M G O L D O C D A E L Z
P N V R U I A D N N F T X N E Y
L L D E M R R X I O D I N E B R
A T N M E E W Z T K O L Q P I U
T Y E O P R T E R D N O B R A C
I B G P W M Y V O N T D O S E R
N E O N E U G I G F A N R C L E
U C R V S I L V E R Y E O M G M
M H D W P C L M N U C P N U U O
S R Y F Q L B X T H Z K J I J X
P R H U R A E H L L C Z D N B Y
X U B E W C K O C E J O I A P G
L F S C L I R W A K S H R T M E
Y L R Z N I V L W C A G Z I E N
S U H B N V U J T I O K E T X Q
T S I E W A M M U N I M U L A L
```

The answers are on page 149.

DIG DEEPER!

* atom
* molecule
* physics
* chemistry

find . . .

Atoms, atoms, everywhere—
In your feet, your hands, your hair;
In the planets, sun, and moon,
Birthday presents, bright balloons.

Lemonade and pumpkin pies,
Bumblebees and butterflies;
Golden rings and sparkling gems,
Acorns, leaves, and flower stems.

Cars and trucks and bikes and swings,
Robin feathers, beaks, and wings;
Hippos, pigs, and hopping frogs,
Water, sand, and lazy fog.

Silverware, the kitchen sink,
Paper clips and loud red ink;
Piano keys and guitar strings—
Atoms make up everything!

Just as atoms are everywhere, so is God. Even though we can't see Him with our eyes, He's in as many places as there are atoms—and more. God is present in everything He made—He's the Creator who breathed the words that brought all those amazing particles into being. But He's also present in space and beyond, in a world that reaches beyond our physical lives—to our hearts. God wants to be more than just some faceless force to you. Through Jesus, you can become even closer to God because you can get to know Him as One who deeply cares about and loves you.

Since God is everywhere at all times, it means that He's always with us. We're never alone. In this life that sometimes seems filled with bumps and bruises, His constant presence and love are a comfort to our hearts.

Thought to remember:

God is always with me.

Additional verses:

1 Kings 8:27; Psalm 139:5; Jeremiah 23:23–24; Acts 17:27–28a; Romans 8:38–39; Ephesians 3:16–19

It's Elementary

If someone asked you to describe gold, you might say it's a shiny yellow metal. You might say gold is soft and heavy and can be shaped into jewelry.

It's not hard to describe gold. At some time in your life, you learned that gold is a metal with certain characteristics—or properties—that set it apart from other metals. We all like to name objects around us and put them in groups. It's a way to become familiar with our world and understand how it works. **Chemists**, scientists who study the substances our world is made of, are no different.

As you may remember, gold is made up of only one kind of atom. Substances such as gold that can't be broken down further into other substances are called *elements*. Every element has a specific number of protons in its atoms. Chemists call this the atomic number. Gold is an element with forty-seven protons in every atom. What's its *atomic number*? Forty-seven. Chemists have arranged elements in a chart by the number of protons they have. This chart, with columns and rows, is called the **periodic** table. You can see this chart by looking up the words *periodic table* or *element* in a dictionary or encyclopedia or on the Internet.

Chemists have discovered that amazing patterns appear when elements are arranged in order by their atomic number. Elements with similar characteristics line up in the same columns or groups. Understanding how one element in the group behaves gives chemists a good idea how others in the same group will behave.

One group of elements is called **alkali** metals. These are found in the very first column at the far left side of the periodic table. They're soft, silvery-colored, and they melt at low temperatures. You might have heard the names of two common alkali metals, *sodium* and *potassium*. These elements fizz and burn when they come into contact with water.

Another group of elements is called **transition** metals. Transition metals tend to be hard and tough. But they can easily be pulled into strands of wire or shaped by

---

chemist: (KEM-ist)

periodic: (peer-ee-ODD-ik)

Scientists have discovered why elements within groups behave in similar ways. Electrons, the tiny particles that whirl around outside the nucleus of an atom, fill up different energy levels. Elements with a similar number of electrons at the outermost energy level behave in similar ways.

alkali: (AL-kuh-lie)

transition: (tran-ZISH-un)

> "Let him who boasts boast about this: that he understands and knows me, that I am the LORD, who exercises kindness, justice and righteousness on earth, for in these I delight," declares the LORD.
>
> JEREMIAH 9:24 (NIV)

In the 1860s a man named **Mendeleev** (men-duh-LAY-uv) began to put together the first periodic table. Mendeleev realized there were elements that hadn't been discovered yet, because there were blank spaces in his chart. By looking at the behavior of the elements around these blank spaces, scientists knew what kind of elements they were looking for. That's how several of these "missing" elements were found.

hammering. Transition metals melt at high temperatures. They're good **conductors** of heat and electricity. Gold is a transition metal. So are copper and iron.

In the column farthest to the right is a group called **noble** gases. Perhaps you've heard of neon. It's a noble gas used to make snazzy colored lights. Neon gives off bright red light when electricity passes through it. Other noble gases in the same column react the same way. Helium, argon, krypton, and **xenon** are also used to create glitzy colors in signs.

Knowing the characteristics of elements in the periodic chart helps us understand them. God also has certain characteristics—or **attributes**—that help us understand Him, too. They help us to know what He's like and how He'll act toward us. God reveals what He's like through nature, the Bible, and His Son, Jesus.

Who is God? What is He like? Here are a few attributes God makes known to us:

* God is **omniscient**. He knows *everything* about us. He knows about everything that goes on around us, too (see Psalm 139:1–5).

* God is just. As the perfect judge, God always knows and does what's right (see Genesis 18:25b).

* God is holy. He is perfectly pure and without sin (see Revelation 4:8, NIV).

* God is merciful. Even though we were separated from God by sin, He treats us with kindness and love and forgives us (see Daniel 9:9, NIV).

* God is loving. He always looks out for our best (see 1 John 4:16; Jeremiah 31:3, NIV).

* God has no beginning or end (see Revelation 4:8, NIV). He's without limits (see Job 11:7–9). There is only one God, and He is in a class by himself (see 2 Chronicles 6:14a)!

Understanding what God is like increases our wonder and awe of Him. It helps us to know and trust Him. Knowing and trusting Him gives us joy, peace, and courage as we journey here on earth.

CONDUCTOR: (KUN-DUCK-ter) a substance that allows heat or electricity to flow through it

NOBLE: (NO-bul)

XENON: (ZEE-non)

attribute: (At-Rih-byute)

omniscient: (ahm-NISH-ent)

To discover more about God's attributes, turn to "Atoms, Atoms Everywhere" on page 11, "Pocket Power" on page 52, "A Handful of Sand" on page 93, "The Reasons for Seasons" on page 109, and "More Faithful Than a Sunrise" on page 112.

Thought to remember:

Understanding what God is like helps me to know Him.

Additional verses:

Deuteronomy 4:39; 2 Samuel 7:22; Psalm 9:10; 14:2; Isaiah 55:8–9; John 17:3; Colossians 1:10b; Hebrews 1:1–3

Check It Out

If you haven't already done so, look up *periodic table* or *element* in a dictionary or encyclopedia or on the Internet. The letters in the middle of the boxes are abbreviations for the names of each element. *Au* is the symbol for gold. Can you find it? Find its atomic number—forty-seven. Gold has forty-seven protons in each atom. Notice how the elements are arranged in order by atomic number. See if you can also find the elements carbon, silver, copper, sodium, and uranium. What are the atomic numbers for these elements?

DIG DEEPER!

* periodic table
* element
* chemistry
* atom

③ Invisible Energy

What do TVs, radios, microwave ovens, and X-ray machines have in common? Their use depends on a special kind of energy. Whether we watch TV, tune in to a radio station, zap food in a microwave, or take X rays of broken bones, we're tapping into a family of energy waves called **electromagnetic radiation.** Where do these waves come from?

The power-packed atom.

As you probably remember, atoms are tiny particles that make up all the matter in our universe. Each atom has a center, or nucleus, made of protons and neutrons. Surrounding the nucleus is a whirling cloud of electrons.

electromagnetic radiation: (ee-LEK-tro-mag-NEH-tik ray-dee-AY-shun)

Now, pretend you're an electron. The distance you are from the nucleus determines how much energy you have. Electrons at energy levels farther away from the nucleus are more pumped up than electrons closer to the nucleus.

To discover more about the friendship between electricity and magnets, turn to "Partners" on page 45.

Sometimes, though, you absorb extra energy. That makes you feel really pumped up, and you jump to a higher energy level, farther away from the nucleus. The more energy you absorb, the farther you jump.

But you don't stay there for long. As you fall back to the level where you began, you give off the extra energy. The farther you fall, the more energy you give off. All members of the electromagnetic wave family— gamma rays, X rays, ultraviolet rays, visible light, infrared rays, microwaves, and radio waves—are produced this way. Gamma rays have the most energy; radio waves have the least.

All electromagnetic waves travel at the speed of light—186,000 miles per second.

> Even though you have not seen Him, you love Him. Though you do not see Him now, you believe in Him. You are filled with a glorious joy that can't be put into words.
>
> 1 PETER 1:8

The word *electromagnetic* gives us more clues about this type of energy. Pretend you're an electron again. Like all electrons, you have a negative electrical charge. This creates an electrical **field** that surrounds you. When you move—and you're always on the go because electrons are always whirling around the nucleus—your electrical field produces a magnetic field. The moving magnetic field then produces a moving electrical field, which produces a moving magnetic field, which produces a moving electrical field . . . and on and on and on. One always produces the other. Quickly changing electrical and magnetic fields allow electromagnetic waves to move

field: (FEELD) the space around an object where the electrical force can push or pull on other objects. Fields also surround magnetic objects.

through space.

Humans have learned to harness electromagnetic energy. We enjoy TVs and radios. X rays give us pictures of our bones, while gamma rays are used to treat cancer. Infrared rays warm us. Ultraviolet rays tan our skin. Except for visible light—the electromagnetic waves we can see—we're constantly surrounded by electromagnetic waves we *can't* see. Most of electromagnetic radiation is invisible to us, but that doesn't change the fact that it's very much a part of our lives.

That's like God, isn't it? Just because we can't see Him doesn't mean He's not there or that He's not active in our lives. How can we be sure God's really there? He reveals himself to us.

The invisible God shows himself through all that He has created. There's only one way the power-packed atom and amazing electromagnetic waves they produce could have come into being—through a wise Creator.

God also gave us a book that teaches about Him. In the Bible we learn about God's love for us . . . about His desire for us to know and be close to Him . . . about Jesus. For thirty-three years the invisible God lived inside a visible body to reveal himself to humans. Now Jesus lives inside all who follow Him.

The invisible God also makes himself known through His effect in our lives. We can't see X rays, but we can see the images they make on film. We can't feel radio waves, but we know they're there because radios pick them up. In a similar way, we can't see or feel God, but we know His love always surrounds us, because He touches our lives. When we pray, He answers. Sometimes He performs miracles in our lives. When we come to Jesus, He gives us new hearts, and then we can see the difference He makes in our lives!

God makes himself known to us through His creation, the Bible, Jesus, and His work in our lives. As we believe what God shows us, the invisible isn't so invisible at all. We can be sure God is with us and that He's active in our lives.

Thought to remember:
I know you are here with me, God, even though I can't see you!

Additional verses:
John 1:18; 14:8–9; 20:29; Romans 1:20;
Colossians 1:15–16; 1 Timothy 1:17; Hebrews 11:1–3, 27

How do we use different forms of electromagnetic radiation?

* Gamma rays are used to treat cancer.

* X rays are used to see inside our bodies because they pass through our flesh but not through our bones.

* Ultraviolet rays give us tans, sunburns . . . and skin cancer.

* Visible light waves are the only electromagnetic waves picked up by our eyes. They make it possible for us to see!

* Infrared rays give us heat. They're also used to detect medical problems and are at work in TV remote controls.

* Microwaves are used to cook and send satellite signals. They're also at work in radar.

* Radio waves are used in TV and radio broadcasting.

List It!

You can't see God, but He is active in your life. Grab a pencil and paper and find a quiet spot. Write down all the ways you've seen God at work in your life. Some clues? Nature, Bible verses, answers to prayer, and changes in your life.

DIG DEEPER!
* atoms
* physics
* electromagnetic waves
* X ray
* ultraviolet light
* infrared light
* light
* radio waves

④ SHINING LIGHT ON LIGHT

Try this multiple-choice question just for fun.

What would happen if all the lights in the world suddenly went out?

a. We'd bump into each other.

b. We'd starve.

c. We'd run out of air.

d. All of the above.

To discover more about waves, turn to "Catch the Wave" on page 35.

If you picked a, b, or c, give yourself a hand. If you picked d, give yourself a standing ovation!

It's easy to understand why we'd bump into each other. We depend on light to see. But would we really starve and run out of air? Yes. Our main source of food and oxygen is green plants. Since plants need light to grow, they'd be in a fix without it—and so would we. There's no doubt about it, we depend on light. In fact, light is such a part of our daily lives that most of us probably don't pay much attention to it.

Have you wondered about light? As you already know, light is a type of electromagnetic radiation that we can see. You know that light is energy. It comes from "excited" electrons that give off energy when they fall from higher ener-

Electromagnetic waves with shorter wavelengths carry more energy. X rays have more energy than ultraviolet waves, which have more energy than visible light, which has more energy than infrared waves.

gy levels to lower ones. And you also may remember that light waves are the result of a connection between electricity and magnetism.

> IN HIS VERY NATURE HE WAS GOD. BUT HE DID NOT THINK THAT BEING EQUAL WITH GOD WAS SOMETHING HE SHOULD HOLD ON TO. INSTEAD, HE MADE HIMSELF NOTHING. HE TOOK ON THE VERY NATURE OF A SERVANT. HE WAS MADE IN HUMAN FORM. HE APPEARED AS A MAN. HE CAME DOWN TO THE LOWEST LEVEL. HE OBEYED GOD COMPLETELY, EVEN THOUGH IT LED TO HIS DEATH . . . ON A CROSS.
>
> PHILIPPIANS 2:6–8

What else do we understand about this bright stuff that lights up our lives? Let's shine some more light on light.

Over the past few centuries, many scientists have believed that light is a wave. Imagine holding on to one end of a piece of rope, and the other end is held by your friend. If you wiggle the rope up and down, a line of waves forms along the rope. The top of one wave to the top of the next is called a *wavelength*. Different types of electromagnetic radiation—such as X rays, light, microwaves, and radio waves—have different *wavelengths*. The distance from the top of one wave to the next is much shorter for X rays than it is for visible light. Understanding that light and other forms of electromagnetic radiation are waves has allowed us to put them to use.

As scientists sought to understand light, they performed experiments that proved light is a wave. But there was a problem. The results in some experiments couldn't be explained by thinking of light as a wave. They could only be explained by describing light as a stream of particles. Another name given to a particle of light is **photon**. Light is a stream of photons, little packets of energy given off by atoms.

photon: (FOE-t'on)

If light is a flow of photons, then what about all the experiments that prove light is a wave? The answer is, light is both. In some experiments light acts like waves, and in others it acts like particles. It's two things at the same time. Light has two natures!

What is true of light is also true of the One who made light, the One who is called the light of the world. Just as light has two natures, so did Jesus. He was God and man at the same time while He walked on earth.

It's hard to understand how Jesus could be God and man at the same time. How could He be without beginning or end, and yet be born? All-powerful, yet at the same time tired and weak? How could He be all-knowing, yet grow in knowledge and understanding? Without needs, yet experience hunger, thirst, and suffering? How could He be the author of life, yet suffer and die?

Whether we completely understand doesn't matter, though. What does matter is that we see why it was a good thing God came to earth as a man. Because Jesus came to earth as a man and lived as we do, we can be sure He knows exactly how we feel at all times. We know that He understands all our struggles because He's been here himself. At the same time, because Jesus was God, He was perfect and without sin. This made it possible for Him to die in our place, to open the way for us to be close to God.

The fact that Jesus was God and man may be hard to understand. But we can be sure that because He was both, He understands us.

Thought to remember:

Jesus was both God and man.

Additional verses:

John 1:1, 14; Romans 1:3–4; 1 Timothy 2:5; Hebrews 2:14, 16–18; 4:15–16

A long time ago scientists argued about the nature of light. In the 1600s, Isaac Newton—who is known for his theory of gravity—studied light. He believed it was made of particles. A Dutch scientist, Christian Huygens (HI-gunz), who lived at the same time, did experiments proving light is a wave.

Explore It!

How can something be more than one thing at the same time? Use an ice-cream cone (without the ice cream!) to explore this idea. Viewed from the side, the ice-cream cone looks like a triangle. Viewed from the end, the ice-cream cone looks like a circle. Which is it, a triangle or a circle? The ice-cream cone is both!

In a similar way, light is not just a wave or particle, but both.

Dig Deeper!

* light
* nature of light
* physics

Marooned in the desert
Beneath a scalding sun,
With no hope of rescue
I feared my life was done.

For stretched out before me
Lay rippled, scorching sand;
Not even cruel buzzards
Flew this forsaken land.

I longed for some shelter—
A tree to offer shade,
A cool splash of water,
An ice-cold lemonade.

When suddenly I spotted
A shimmering, shiny pool,
I could almost taste it—
Fresh water, blue and cool.

I crawled toward the water
With the last of my might,
But before I could reach it,
It vanished from my sight!

mirage: (mih-razh)

You've probably seen a **mirage** before—a shimmering pool of water over hot sand or a heated road. How does nature play tricks on our eyes, forming an image of water where there isn't any?

refraction: (re-FRAK-shun)

It uses **refraction**, the bending of light. Here's how it works:

In the case of a desert mirage, the air temperature directly above sand is heated to a higher temperature than air higher up. Light coming from the sky travels through the cool air before passing into the warm air near the sand. As it passes from cool air to warm air, the light travels more quickly. Why? Because warm air has fewer air molecules to get in the way and slow down the light rays. This causes the light rays

> **Heaven and earth will pass away. But my words will never pass away.**
>
> MARK 13:31

optical illusion:
(OP-tih-kul
ih-LOO-zhun)
something that's
misleading to
your eyes

To discover more
about refraction
and rainbows, turn
to "Rainbow of
Promises" on
page 27.

to gradually bend away from the ground and up toward your eyes, instead of traveling straight into the ground. That's how you see the blue of the sky—or what looks like a pool of water—on the sand.

Refraction of light through varying air temperatures also creates other **optical illusions**. When cold air is trapped beneath hot air as it sometimes is over the ocean, you might see a ship plus an upside-down image of it hovering over the water. When light travels through layers of cold and hot air above sand, hot asphalt, or a hot stove, you can see air shimmer, or wiggle.

Light also bends when it passes through other substances, such as water or glass. As you might guess, light travels more slowly through water than air. That's why water looks shallower than it actually is . . . why a fish seems closer to the surface and nearer to the shore . . . why your friend's underwater legs appear stubby.

When refraction is in action, things aren't really as they appear to be! The same can be true for us. Our feelings often refract the truth about our lives and God. Perhaps . . .

* you feel as if you don't have any friends. You think you're unlovable. What's the truth? God says: "I delight in you. I love you more than you can imagine" (see Zephaniah 3:17; Ephesians 3:17–19).
* you're at the bottom of your class. Perhaps kids never seem to pick you for their teams. You feel worthless and like giving up. What's the truth? God says: "You're worth so much to me that I gave my Son for you. You're complete in Him. You have everything you need in Jesus to live your life on earth" (see Romans 8:31–32; Philippians 4:19; Colossians 2:9–10).
* you feel as if you can never please your parents. Now you think you're not good enough for God, either. What's the truth? God says: "Because you believe in Jesus, I will never, ever condemn you. You're acceptable to me, even if you mess up. I love you just the way I made you" (see Romans 5:8; 8:1, 33–34).
* there are problems in your home. God feels far, far away. What's the truth? God says: "I'm here for you. I promise I won't ever leave. No matter how confusing things are in your life, you can't be separated from my love" (see Romans 8:38; Hebrews 13:5b).

Here are more fun facts about refraction:

* The sun rises a few minutes later than we think. As light travels through layers of the atmosphere, it bends, bringing us a view of the sun before it's actually there. At sunset we enjoy the sun a few minutes after it goes down.
* The archerfish shoots bullets of water to capture insects. How does this fish overcome the bending of light from water to air in order to hit its tricky target? Perhaps through trial and error.
* Sound waves are like light—they also change speed and bend as they travel through different air temperatures and substances. A cold layer of air trapped near the ground causes sound waves to curve toward the ground and the listener. That's why sound carries better in the cool of night.

CHECK It Out!

Check out for yourself how light bends as it travels from air to glass and into water. Fill a clear drinking glass with water. Stick a pencil in the water, leaning it against the lip of the glass. How does the pencil look when viewed from the side? The underwater part of the pencil no longer lines up with the part that sticks into the air. Viewed from above, the pencil also appears shorter than it really is. Light coming from the pencil refracts as it travels from water to air.

TRy It!

To amaze your family and friends with this refraction-action activity, you'll need an **opaque** (oh-PAKE) bowl (one you can't see through), a coin, and a glass of water.

Tell a friend to sit at a table. Place the coin at the bottom of the bowl, as close to the side as possible. Set the bowl on the table and move the bowl away from your friend until the coin is out of sight. Now pour water into the bowl. The coin will reappear, even though your friend hasn't moved an inch!

DIG DEEPER!

* light
* refraction
* physics

Just as light produces optical illusions through refraction, our feelings can bend the truth and trick us into thinking things about ourselves that aren't true. Don't let your feelings tell you that you're not special and that God doesn't love you. Know what God says about you through the Bible. Then, no matter how you feel, believe Him!

Thought to remember:

No matter how I feel, I believe what *God* says about me.

Additional verses:

Psalm 119:105; John 17:17; Romans 1:17; 2 Timothy 3:16; Hebrews 11:1, 6; James 1:6

6 Riddle of Light

Here's a riddle:

What comes out at night and in the day,
Is often black, but also gray?

What is often big, but can be small,
Is often short, but can be tall?
A shadow!

Are all shadows black or gray? You might be surprised to find that some are purple, some are blue, and some may even be dark green.

Whether we notice or not, shadows tag along with us just about everywhere we go. What causes these gray images to appear?

To make a shadow, two ingredients are needed.

The first is light. We live in a world bathed in the bright stuff. During the day most of it comes from the sun. But even at night the stars, the moon, and electric bulbs shine all around us.

The second ingredient for a shadow is an object that gets in the way of light. Put a solid object in front of light, and you will cast a shadow on a wall, the floor, a sidewalk, the door.

That's because light travels in straight lines. When light hits an object, the light is blocked. The result is a shadow—a dark area that lacks light on the other side of the object.

Perhaps you've noticed that some shadows are dark and crisp, while others are gray and fuzzy. A black shape with sharp edges is created when not a single ray of light gets through. It's called an **umbra**. A softer, grayer shadow, or **penumbra**, is only a partial shadow. Some light is able to fill in behind the object.

> HOW PRICELESS YOUR FAITHFUL LOVE IS! IMPORTANT AND ORDINARY PEOPLE ALIKE FIND SAFETY IN THE SHADOW OF YOUR WINGS.
>
> PSALM 36:7

umbra: (UM-bruh)

penumbra: (Peh-NUM-bruh)

The closer an object is to the place where its shadow falls, such as a wall, the more distinct its shadow is likely to be. But even a well-defined shadow is often surrounded by a fuzzy halo. This two-part shadow—with both umbra and penumbra—takes shape the farther an object moves away from the wall and the closer it gets to the light source. The closer an object moves to the light source, the fuzzier its shadow grows, until all we see is a gray penumbra.

Can you guess where we get the word **umbrella**? The first part of the word looks a lot like **umbra**, doesn't it? Umbra is the Latin word for **shade**. Umbrellas give us shade, or a shadow. Under the shadow of umbrellas, we find relief from rain or sun!

Check It Out!

Check out how shadows behave. You will need

* a desk lamp that directs light in one direction

* a large sheet of white paper

* a large book

Turn on the lamp in a darkened room. Place your hand between the light and paper. How do shadows change as your hand moves closer to the paper? To the lamp? Do you see the dark umbra and lighter penumbra?

Now hold the book in front of the lamp. How are the umbra and penumbra different from the shadows of your hand?

Make It!

Did you know shadows can be used to tell time? Make a sundial. All you need is a six- to twelve-inch-long stick and a sunny day. Poke your stick straight into the ground where the sun shines on it all day. Every hour visit the sundial. How does the shadow change as the sun travels across the sky? Compare the shadow with the time on your watch. At what time of day is the shadow shortest?

Dig Deeper!

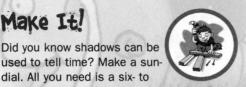

* light
* physics for kids
* shadows

The distance an object is from its shadow and the light source change the way the shadow appears. So do the size of the object and the size of the light source. Bigger objects cast shadows with bigger umbras, or deep black areas. But as the size of the light increases, more rays of light can get past the object—the black umbra shrinks, and the gray penumbra grows.

Whether we understand that shadows have umbras, penumbras, or both, they can still be scary to us. That's especially true of big, moving shadows in the middle of the night! But here's another way to look at shadows. When we're outside and the sun's hot light burns down on us, all we think about is finding shade. What's another name for the shade of a tree or a rock or a cloud? A shadow!

In our lives, we also have troubles that beat down on us like the hot, hot sun. We search for relief in many ways. Perhaps we try to make the problem go away or try to run from it. But that can be like trying to make the sun go away. It can be like trying to escape from the sun's hot rays when there is no place to hide. What do we do when we have a hot problem?

The Lord wants us to run to Him. He offers us relief and comfort close by His side, in the cool of His shade . . . in the shadow of His wings.

There's no one and nothing more powerful than God. In fact, one of His names, the Lord Almighty, tells us He is all-powerful. There's no one who is more faithful or loving than He is, either. Our powerful, loving God can give us peace and rest deep inside our hearts, even in the midst of any problem.

Whenever you encounter a hot problem in your life, take cover in the shadow of the Almighty. You'll find comfort and relief.

Thought to remember:
God gives me comfort in the shadow of His wings.

Additional verses:
Psalm 17:8 (NIV); 57:1; 63:7; 91:1, 4; 121:5–8

7 A CHORUS OF COLOR

Can you imagine a world without color?

A colorless world would be a world without rainbows, the deep blue sea, color pictures, and color TVs.

Not only would life seem dull, but what would you call oranges? Or violets? Or plums?

How would you express love without silly poems like "Roses are red, violets are blue"?

Passing a test with "flying colors" would be unheard of.

On the other hand, if you missed most of the answers, at least you couldn't turn "red in the face" with embarrassment. And a friend's perfect grade couldn't make you "green with envy." Nor would your mother constantly remind you to "eat your greens."

What makes our world sing with a chorus of laughing yellows, bashful blues, and graceful greens? The secret lies in light.

prism: (PRIZ-um) a clear triangular wedge of glass or crystal that bends white light into the colors of the rainbow

In the mid-1600s a man named Isaac Newton focused sunlight on a **prism**. The light entered the prism, and when it came out the other side, it was split into the colors of the rainbow. When Newton aimed the rainbow at a second prism, the colors recombined into a ray of white light. Newton had discovered that the sun's white light is made of red, orange, yellow, green, blue, indigo, and violet colors.

> **Thanks be to God for his indescribable gift!**
> 2 CORINTHIANS 9:15

Each color has a different wavelength. Red has a slightly longer wavelength than orange. Orange has a slightly longer wavelength than yellow. Yellow has a slightly longer wavelength than green—you get the picture! Violet has the shortest wavelength.

The colors we see are from wavelengths of light that strike an object and bounce, or reflect, back to our eyes. Blueberries look blue because they reflect mostly blue wavelengths. The other colors are **absorbed**. What color do you think strawberries reflect?

absorb: (ab-ZORB) to take in and hold on to

We see colors because light reflects back to our eyes. Just what is it about our eyes that enable us to detect different colors? Nerve endings at the back of our eyes, called cones, are designed to pick up color. We have three types of cones. Each is sensitive

25

Cones pick up color and detail, but they don't work well in dim light. For night sight, our eyes are equipped with rods. Rods don't relay messages of color. That's why we don't see color at night. Some people are color-blind. They're born without one of the three types of cones. Often, color-blind people can tell blues and yellows apart, but they confuse reds and greens. Very few people see no colors at all. Color blindness is more common in boys than girls.

TRY It!

If you don't already have one, buy an inexpensive prism from a gift or craft store. Set the prism where sunlight can shine on it. As light enters the prism, it bends and separates into different wavelengths. That's what causes the colors of the rainbow to emerge. Enjoy this amazing display of colors!

DIG DEEPER!

★ light
★ color
★ optics
★ Isaac Newton

to long, medium, or short wavelengths of light. Only certain cones respond to red, which send a signal to the brain to see red. What do you think happens when we look at a piece of white paper? All the cones respond and we see white.

Why would God bother to create light formed of a chorus of color, and give us eyes to see them?

Perhaps God gave us a dazzling world because it's one way for us to learn about Him, the heavenly Artist. Color reflects His beauty. Variety reveals His attention to detail.

Color also shows our Creator's goodness. He's a thoughtful Father who gives us an amazing world to delight in.

Color also shows His care. God is a helpful Father who provides color so we can function in the world He designed. Can you think of some practical ways that color helps us?

Most of all, color gives us a hint about God's love for us. He's a loving Father who delights to shower His children with good gifts. His choice to give us the gift of color isn't surprising when we stop to think about His willingness to give us the gift of His Son, Jesus. This one gift is greater than all others. It's **indescribable**! **Unspeakable**! Jesus brings full "color" into our lives, which are hopeless and dull without Him.

Color brings zing; it adds pizzazz. To experience the richness of the chorus of color, all we need to do is open our eyes and appreciate the world we live in. When we do, we may notice more than pretty pinks and outrageous oranges. Our eyes could also be opened to the God who made colors, who cares about us and wants us to know Him.

Thought to remember:
God reveals himself to me through the gift of color.

Additional verses:
Genesis 1:3, 31; Ecclesiastes 3:11a; Ezekiel 34:26; John 10:10b; Romans 8:32; 1 Timothy 6:17; James 1:17 (NIV)

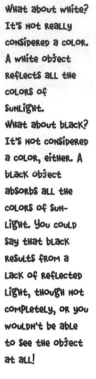

What about white? It's not really considered a color. A white object reflects all the colors of sunlight. What about black? It's not considered a color, either. A black object absorbs all the colors of sunlight. You could say that black results from a lack of reflected light, though not completely, or you wouldn't be able to see the object at all!

indescribable: (in-din-SCRY-buh-bul) beyond description

unspeakable: (un-SPEAK-uh-bul) cannot be put into words

8 Rainbow of Promises

You know those special days in your life—

Christmas, birthdays, family vacations, the last day of school? Aren't they different from ordinary days? They're fun, and often—like brightly wrapped gifts—filled with surprises. They make you feel special and bring you smiles.

One mystery in nature can turn any ordinary day into a special one. Because this mystery appears only under certain conditions, it delights and surprises us. Like a gift, it can make us feel special and brings us smiles.

What can do all that?

A rainbow.

To understand how these brightly colored arcs appear, let's review a few fun facts about light. The white light from the sun is a combination of different colors: red, orange, yellow, green, blue, indigo, and violet. Light travels as a wave, and each color has a different wavelength. Red has the longest wavelength. Violet has the shortest. A final fun fact is this: When light travels from air to glass or water, it bends, or refracts. Red wavelengths bend the least; violet wavelengths bend the most. The differences in bending explain why sunlight splits into different colors when it travels through a prism . . . or a raindrop.

It's easy to remember all the colors of the rainbow. Take the first letter of each color and put them together to spell the name ROY G. BIV.

> GOD isn't a mere man. He can't lie. He isn't a human being. He doesn't change his mind. He speaks, and then He acts. He makes a promise, and then He keeps it.
>
> NUMBERS 23:19

Imagine a stormy afternoon. The lightning has ended, so it's safe to go outside. In one part of the sky, the clouds have cleared and the sun is shining. Now *turn your back to the sun*. Face the section of sky where it's still raining and—can we have a drum roll, please?—there's a rainbow! Here's how it happens:

Light from the sun hits the upper part of each raindrop. As it enters a raindrop, the light bends, separating into the colors of a rainbow. The light then bounces off the back of the raindrop and travels to the bottom, where it bends again as it leaves the raindrop. This final bend increases the separation of colors to give us lively reds, oranges, yellows, greens, blues, and violets. These bright bands of color that stretch across the sky are also the result of just the right angle of sunlight, water droplets, and your eyes.

It's amazing how rainbows form. It's also amazing that God speaks to us through them.

Here's a rainbow of trivia:

* If you were to see a rainbow from an airplane, it might look like a full circle.

* Everyone sees a different rainbow because their eyes receive light from different raindrops.

* Double rainbows make rainbow days doubly special! A second, faint rainbow sometimes appears above the brighter one below. This upper arch forms in a similar way to the lower one, but the light bounces off the inside of the raindrop *twice*, instead of once. Because of this extra bounce, the colors are reversed. Violet ends up on top, red on the bottom. This rainbow is dim because some of the light also refracts out the back of the rainbow.

Make It!

If you have a sunny day and a hose with a nozzle, you can create your own rainbow. With your back to the sun, set the nozzle to produce a fine spray of water, and **voilà** (vwah-LAH), a rainbow appears! If at first you don't succeed, simply move the spray left, right, up, or down.

DIG DEEPER!

* rainbow
* light
* color spectrum
* optics
* physics

Long ago, God used a flood to destroy life on earth because people's hearts thought only of evil. But cradled safely inside an ark, a man named Noah, his family, and every kind of animal survived. After the flood, God promised that He would never again destroy life on earth with a flood. The rainbow is a reminder of His promise.

God has never broken that promise, and He never will. How can we be sure He never will? God is Truth, so what He says is true. He can't lie. We can depend on Him to keep His promise.

Rainbows also remind us that God keeps *all* His promises. He gives us a rainbow of promises throughout the Bible. They're all gifts. God gives them to us out of love, and when we open them we feel special. They bring delight to our lives. Sometimes they even surprise us.

If you've never looked for God's "rainbows" before, here's a start. God promised He would

* send a Savior to our world (see John 3:16).
* send His Spirit to teach you (see John 14:26).
* never leave you (see Hebrews 13:5).
* meet *all* your needs through Jesus (see Philippians 4:19).
* be your Father (see 2 Corinthians 6:18).
* give rest and peace to your heart (see John 14:27).

The next time you see a rainbow, remember the amazing way it formed from sunlight and water droplets. Remember that God gives many promises, and none of them can be broken. Remember that you can count on Him.

Thought to remember:

I can count on God to keep His promises.

Additional verses:

Joshua 21:45; Psalm 33:4, 9; 145:13; 2 Corinthians 1:20a; 2 Peter 1:3–4

9 A See-Through You!

Look through a window.

What do you see on the other side? Now look through a wall. Look through a wall? "Impossible!" you say. Why can you see through windows but not walls? The obvious answer is, windows let light through. Windows are clear, while wood and plaster aren't.

If we dig a little deeper, we can learn why most windows are **transparent**, letting light pass through in straight lines so that we can see what's on the other side. We can discover why wood and plaster don't. To understand, we'll need to travel to the place where the action happens. Shrink way down past the size of an ant, past the size of a grain of sugar, all the way to a world invisible to the eye of humans—the world of the atom.

> Let us come near to God with an honest and true heart.
>
> HEBREWS 10:22

Now watch what happens when a wave of light strikes glass. The atoms in the glass begin to **vibrate**. This sets up sort of a chain reaction. One atom absorbs the light energy and passes it to another atom, which also absorbs the energy and passes it to another atom. One after the other, atoms pass light energy through the glass until it comes out the other side.

Can you think of see-through materials besides glass? Water is one. Liquid wax, some plastics, and the crystal clear skin of the glass frog, which lives in the rain forest, are others.

Even though light energy is passed from atom to atom, some of it scatters. That's especially true for extra thick glass that doesn't give us a clear view of what's on the other side. Too much light scatters on the way through. An object that scatters light so that we can't see through it clearly is **translucent**. Can you think of other materials that let only part of the light through? Here are a few to get you started: solid wax, some seashells, tissue paper, your fingernail and skin, frosted and colored glass, and many plastics.

Some materials—such as walls—don't let *any* light through at all. The atoms in these objects absorb light energy or reflect it back toward the source of light. None of the light is passed through to the other side. Objects that don't let any light through are **opaque**. Look around. Many opaque objects surround you. Wood, metal, stones,

How well you can see through an object sometimes depends on temperature. Refrigerated butter is opaque. But when butter is heated and melts, it becomes clear. Wax is translucent before it melts and becomes transparent. Ice is also translucent before it melts and turns crystal clear.

List It!

Grab a pencil and piece of paper! At the top of the paper, write headings for three columns: Transparent, Translucent, and Opaque. Now explore your world to discover objects that fit under each column. If you have trouble deciding which column an object fits under, you might find it helpful to hold it up to a window or light. Can you see through it clearly, does only a little bit of light shine through, or does the object block light completely?

Here are some ideas to jump-start your list: plastic wrap, aluminum foil, waxed paper, leaves, petals, bark, fabrics, and foods.

Check It Out!

Read about Adam and Eve (Genesis 2:15–25 and 3:1–13), the first man and woman to hide from God. Think about these questions as you read:

✦ What was Adam and Eve's relationship with God like before they ate fruit from the Tree of Knowledge of Good and Evil?

✦ How did Adam and Eve hide from God after they ate the fruit?

✦ Why do you think Adam and Eve hid?

DIG DEEPER!

✦ light
✦ physics for kids

some plastics, and most parts of our bodies are just a few.

For the most part, our bodies are opaque to light. But did you know there's a part of us that can be transparent? When it comes to how we communicate with God, we can be open and honest—we can let light shine through us.

Jesus made it possible for us to be close to God. But sometimes we're afraid to come close; we're afraid to be transparent with God. Perhaps it's because we have the wrong idea about Him. We're afraid He's just like some people who always expect us to be perfect, who become angry when we mess up. Or perhaps there's a secret tucked away in our hearts that we're ashamed of. We're sure God could never forgive us for *that*. We think that if we're really, really open with God about ourselves, there's no way He'll accept us. So we hide. We become opaque.

Well, guess what? You can relax! God knows that none of us are going to be perfect. If we were, we wouldn't need Jesus. He's the One who makes us perfect. And those secrets? He already knows all about them.

God's desire is for you to trust Him like you would trust a loving father. He wants you to come near and talk heart to heart with Him—even about the things you're embarrassed about. He wants you to let the light of His love shine right through to your heart.

Go to God just as you are. Draw near and be a see-through you!

Thought to remember:

I can be completely open and honest with God!

Additional verses:

Psalm 32:1–5; 62:8 (NIV); 139:1–4, 11–12; Jeremiah 31:3 (NIV); Hebrews 10:22; 1 John 1:7

Have you ever taken a walk on a frosty day?

If so, perhaps you discovered the delight of seeing sparkles everywhere. They're sprinkled over fields, on chain link fences, even along tree branches. It's as if some invisible hand powdered the world with the dust of diamonds, rubies, emeralds, and sapphires.

The sparkles that dazzle us don't come from jewels, of course. They're millions and millions of tiny mirrors, tiny crystals of ice, each with a smooth, flat surface. When sunlight hits the face of a smooth, flat ice crystal, it bounces off, or reflects. That's what causes ordinary fields to dance with lights.

A man-made mirror works the same way. It's smooth and flat to reflect nearly every bit of light that hits it. A ray of light strikes the mirror at a certain angle and bounces *away* at a matching angle— like a basketball that bounces away from you when you throw it at the floor. Since a mirror is smooth, the light reflects in a uniform way so that it enters our eyes just as if the object we see in the mirror is there itself.

That's why a plane, or flat, mirror never lies. When you look at a plane mirror, you see a twin—a reversed twin—that has the same smile or bad hair that you do! The image coming from the mirror is the same size. It even looks as if it's as far behind the mirror as you are in front of it. But it's not really. Your brain just thinks it is.

Curved mirrors create a slightly different type of image than plane mirrors. One type, the **convex** mirror, bulges like the outside of a balloon. If you look into a convex mirror, what will you see? Light waves strike the bulged surface and spread out, so you see a shrunken, slightly misshapen image of yourself. You also see a wider area around you than normal.

Another type of curved mirror, called the **concave** mirror, has a surface that's scooped out, like the inside of a balloon. If you hold a concave mirror close to your face, what will you see? A magnified version of yourself! As you move the concave mirror

---

Why don't we see our reflections on paper or walls? These surfaces are uneven. Light rays strike them and scatter in many directions.

convex: (KON-VEKS) curves outward, like the back of a spoon

Convex mirrors are used on large trucks and campers to give a wide view of the side of the vehicle. This kind of mirror makes objects look farther away than they really are, so drivers must be careful.

concave: (KON-KAVE) curves inward, like the inside of a spoon

---

You created the deepest parts of my being. You put me together inside my mother's body. How you made me is amazing and wonderful. I praise you for that. What you have done is wonderful. I know that very well.

PSALM 139:13–14

Mirrors didn't always look the way they do today. The earliest ones, dating back 1,300 years before Jesus was born, were made of polished brass and bronze. Glass backed by shiny metal—similar to the mirrors we use today—first appeared in Italy, during the 1300s.

ExPLORe It!

You know how you look in a plane mirror. But how does your reflection appear in convex and concave mirrors? To explore it, you'll need a large shiny spoon from your kitchen. First turn the spoon so that the outer—or convex—surface faces you. Do you look small and distorted?

Now flip the spoon around so that the inner—or concave—surface faces you. Are you upside-down? You'll have to bring the spoon right up to your eye in order to see yourself magnified and right side up.

DIG DEEPER!

* mirrors
* light
* physics

away from your face, your image will turn upside down.

Most of us depend on mirrors to tell us whether or not we're having a bad hair day. But for some of us, checking out our reflection is upsetting. We might as well be looking into a curved mirror that deforms our image. Our nose is too fat or too pointy. Our eyes are too squinty, and our mouth, too big. Our hair is too thick or too thin, too straight or too wavy. And our skin? Too light or too dark. We're convinced we're too fat, too skinny, too short, too tall, too this or too that. Our reflection in a mirror can bring major disappointment that turns on the tears.

If you cringe every time you look in the mirror, there's hope. But it doesn't come with covering up or changing the features you don't like about yourself.

What *is* the answer?

Knowing that the person you see in the mirror is loved by God. Believing that when He designed you, He didn't make any mistakes. Every detail about you—your face, your hair, your skin, and your body—was specially hand-picked by Him. He's pleased with the way He made you. He thinks you're wonderful.

When you know—really know in your heart—how special you are to God, then you can be satisfied with yourself. You can stop worrying about what others think about the way you look. That kind of confidence puts a smile on your face—and in your reflection, too.

Thought to remember:
God handpicked the features of my body. I am special.

Additional verses:
Psalm 17:8 (NIV); 40:5 (NIV); Isaiah 43:6b–7; 62:4; Jeremiah 31:3 (NIV); Ephesians 3:17–19

HeRe'S How you caN RememBeR tHe DiffeReNce betweeN coNvex aND coNcave: THe SecoND SyLLaBle of coNcave iS cave. CaveS cuRve iNwaRD.

Throughout history many discoveries have led to inventions that make our lives easier. Hundreds of years ago, just such a discovery was made. Some people believe it took place when a glassblower noticed that objects look larger when viewed through a piece of curved glass. This was a discovery with huge possibilities. By the late 1200s glasses had been invented. Today we call a piece of curved glass or plastic a **lens**. If you wear glasses or contacts, then you appreciate how important corrective lenses are! But even if you don't depend on glasses or contacts to see, lenses still affect your life. Microscopes, cameras, binoculars, telescopes, magnifying glasses, and movie projectors all grew out of the glassblower's discovery.

lens: (LENZ)

The word lens comes from a Latin word for lentil, the pea plant seed that has a rounded shape.

To discover more about refraction, turn to "Refraction Action" on page 20.

How do lenses work? As you already know, when light enters glass it bends, or refracts. When light strikes a lens, it does the same thing. How the light bends depends on what kind of curve the lens has.

One kind of lens looks like an oval when viewed from the side. It bulges out at the middle and narrows at the top and bottom. That's why it's called a convex lens. Light rays that pass through this type of lens bend toward each other. At a certain point on the other side of the lens, light rays come together to form an image. A magnifying glass is a convex lens. Objects seen through a magnifying glass appear larger; details are more distinct.

> THERE IS ONLY ONE LAWGIVER AND JUDGE. HE IS THE ONE WHO IS ABLE TO SAVE LIFE OR DESTROY IT. BUT WHO ARE YOU TO JUDGE YOUR NEIGHBOR?
>
> JAMES 4:12

Another kind of lens has sides that curve in when viewed from the side. This lens looks like a fat capital "I" with a half-moon carved out of each side. The top and bottom are wider than the middle. That's why this type of lens is called a concave lens. Light rays that pass through a concave lens bend away—or spread out—from each other.

Both kinds of lenses are used in corrective glasses and contact lenses. If you have normal eyesight, light rays reflect off an object and focus on the **retina** at the back of the eye. But sometimes the image doesn't quite reach the retina. That's what happens if you're nearsighted, or have trouble seeing things that are far away. Most likely your eyeball is longer than normal. Your eye can't adjust its own lens enough to make the

retina: (REH-tih-nuh)

How does your eye focus the light rays that enter it? They are focused mainly by the cornea (KORE-nee-uh), a clear layer at the front of your eyeball. From there, light passes through the pupil (the dark hole in the middle of your eye) to a built-in lens that focuses the light even more. Tiny muscles hooked to the lens adjust it, making the lens fatter or thinner, depending on how close the object is.

Discover It!

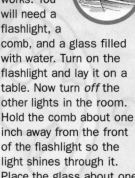

See for yourself how a convex lens works. You will need a flashlight, a comb, and a glass filled with water. Turn on the flashlight and lay it on a table. Now turn *off* the other lights in the room. Hold the comb about one inch away from the front of the flashlight so the light shines through it. Place the glass about one inch away from the front of the comb. Do the light beams come together on the other side of the glass?

DIG DEEPER!

* lens
* optics
* light
* eye

image fall on the retina. Instead, the light rays from the object you're looking at come together in front of the retina. A concave lens helps light focus right on the retina to give you a clear picture.

The opposite is true if far away objects appear crisp and clear, but everything up close is fuzzy. In that case, you're farsighted. Your eyeball is most likely too short, so light rays don't have a chance to form an image by the time they reach the retina. What kind of lens rescues farsighted people from blurry vision? That's right! A convex lens brings the image together at just the right spot.

Just as our physical eyes sometimes need correction, so do the eyes of our hearts. When we condemn others and point out their faults, we're judging them. It may seem that we see their faults clearly. But when it comes to judging others, we must always remember that the eyes of our hearts can be out of focus. Our hearts can be nearsighted or farsighted. We need to put on the corrective lenses that help us see God, others, and ourselves more clearly. Spiritual corrective lenses come from the Bible. They help us to see these things:

* God is the only true Judge. Only He can see inside a person's heart and know the truth. What gives us—mere humans—the right to put ourselves in God's place? (see Romans 2:2, NIV; James 4:11–12).

* We're guilty of the same things (see Matthew 7:3–5; Romans 2:1, NIV).

* Judging others brings God's judgment on us (see Luke 6:37).

* Each of us needs God's mercy, kindness, and forgiveness, so how can we look down on somebody else? (see Romans 2:4, NIV).

* God values and greatly loves each of us. Sometimes we put down others because we don't feel good about ourselves. Knowing and believing what God thinks about us helps put everything in focus (see Jeremiah 31:3, NIV; Zechariah 2:8b).

It's no fun to grumble about others. If you find yourself in the mood to criticize, put on corrective lenses for the eyes of your heart.

Thought to remember:
When you're tempted to judge someone else, remember the mercy God shows you.

Additional verses:
Matthew 7:1–2; Romans 2:1–4 (NIV); 14:4, 10–12

12 Catch the Wave

Take a ride on the wild side.

Grab a surfboard and come on! It's time to catch a wave.

We paddle our boards into the ocean where the water's deep and the waves promise to grow tall. The water swells. Gliding into position before the wave arrives, we jump to our feet just as it rises beneath us and pushes us toward shore.

If we're good, we'll steady our boards just below the top of the wave. If we're really good, we'll pull 360s or ride the face of the wave like a roller coaster. Wahoo! Ride 'em! We'll tame this bronco, staying afloat till it runs out of energy and breaks near shore.

Where do waves come from?

Waves are born when wind disturbs the surface of the sea and produces a ripple. As the wind continues to push against this tiny wave, it increases in size until it's large enough to ride.

Even though it seems as if we're surfing on a wall of moving water, the water isn't what moves at all. It's energy that moves. The energy just disturbs the water as it moves toward land.

The same is true of all waves—it's energy that moves from one point to another. A sound wave is energy that's picked up by our ears. A light wave is energy that's picked up by our eyes.

While you skimmed the sea, you might have noticed that the waves in front and behind you look a lot like each other. That's because all waves have certain characteristics. Every wave has a high point, called a **crest**. The very lowest point in the dip of the wave is called a **trough**.

Now let's towel off and head to a pond, where we'll check out another characteristic of waves. To make our own waves, let's drop a pebble into this still water. This creates a circle of ripples that looks like a target. What happens when we drop *two* pebbles near each other?

A different pattern forms where the waves run into each other. When two waves meet, we call it **interference**.

Picture the top of a wave, or crest, coming together with the bottom of a wave, or

crest: (RHymes with Rest)

trough: (TROFF)

Another characteristic of waves is diffraction (DIH-FRAK-SHun). A wave spreads out as it passes through a small opening or by the edge of an obstacle.

> May the God who gives endurance and encouragement give you a spirit of unity among yourselves as you follow Christ Jesus, so that with one heart and mouth you may glorify the God and Father of our Lord Jesus Christ.
>
> ROMANS
> 15:5–6(NIV)

The energy of a wave needs a substance for it to travel through. Ocean waves travel through water. Sound waves travel through air, water, or land. But light waves are different—they don't need a substance to carry them. Because they're electromagnetic waves, they can travel through empty space.

trough. Where a crest and a trough meet, they cancel each other out to produce level areas in the water. A crest plus a trough causes **destructive** interference. These waves are "out of step" with each other.

interference: (in-ter-FEAR-ents)

destructive: (din-STRUCK-tiv)

Now picture a crest coming together with another crest. These areas form high points in the ripples. Why? Because the two crests add together to form one bigger crest. And what happens when two troughs overlap? These create low points in the ripples because together, the two troughs form one deeper trough. One crest plus another crest—or one trough plus another trough—causes **constructive** interference. These waves are "in step" with each other. They strengthen or build each other up.

What happens to waves after they overlap? They pass through one another and continue on their way.

constructive: (kun-STRUCK-tiv)

Does interference occur with sound and light waves, too? Yes. And you could say that it happens in our lives, as well.

In a way, our lives are like waves. Every day we send out ripples that affect everyone we come in contact with. Are we in or out of step with those we mingle with every day?

Our attitudes cause destructive interference when we hurt others. Fighting, temper tantrums, outbursts of anger, and being just plain mean are clearly hurtful behaviors. But even pride, jealousy, **backbiting**, and separating into **cliques** harm our friends and family. Our bad behaviors don't just harm others. They harm us, as well.

backbite: to say mean things about someone when they're not with you

clique: (CLICK) a group of people that sticks closely together but keeps others out

We can't control the behaviors of someone else, but we are responsible for our own behavior. We don't have to be out of step with those around us. We can be in step by following the Spirit of God. His love, patience, kindness, gentleness, and goodness spread through us to others. Just as two crests or two troughs coming together build and strengthen, so our constructive behaviors can also support others and build them up.

And God values that, especially between people who believe in Jesus. That's because

* He wants His children to get along. Each of us is the apple of His eye. That's like being His favorite (see Psalm 17:8, NIV).

* we're one with Jesus and with each other. So how we treat others is also how we're treating Jesus (see Matthew 25:35–40; Acts 9:3, NIV; Acts 9:3, NIV; Colossians 1:27).

★ it brings glory to God (see Romans 15:5, NIV).

Every day we can be in step with others to build them up. Just as constructive waves strengthen each other, when we help others it's good for us, too!

Thought to remember:

I want to be in step with others.

Additional verses:

Psalm 133:1; Proverbs 10:12; Mark 9:50; Ephesians 4:3–6; Colossians 3:12–15

Explore It!

See for yourself how the energy of a wave moves through a substance, disturbing it. Mark a spot on a long rope with a marker. Tie one end of the rope to a solid object, or have a friend hold one end. Now give the rope a shake up and down so that it wiggles. Is the spot still at the same place on the rope? Yes. Pieces of rope don't move from one end to the other. Energy does. The movement of energy causes waves, or disturbances, in the rope.

Dig Deeper!

★ waves
★ physics
★ light
★ sound
★ surfing

Shh. Sit quietly for a few seconds and listen.

What do you hear?

Perhaps you heard a sparrow sing, the telephone ring, the wind in the trees, a cough, or a sneeze. Or perhaps you heard a baby cry, your best friend sigh, the caw of a crow, the radio. Perhaps you heard an echo, echo, echo.

We live in a world filled with sounds. They bring us pleasure, warn us about danger, and pass along information. Noisy sounds can annoy us. Where do sounds come from?

Every sound begins with a vibration, something that moves back and forth very quickly. An example is a rubber band pulled tight between two fingers and plucked like a musical instrument. Or put your hand on your throat and say, "This is fun." Did you feel your vocal chords vibrate?

The vibrations from your vocal chords disturb the air all around you. Moving through the air in waves, this energy is passed from air molecule to air molecule until it reaches your ears.

Sound waves travel fifteen times faster through steel, and four times faster in water, than air.

If sound waves can pass from air molecule to air molecule, then can they pass through the molecules of other materials, too? If you've ever tapped the side of a pool while underwater, then you know that sounds travel even better through water than through air.

> The sheep listen to his voice. He calls his own sheep by name and leads them out. When he has brought all of his own sheep out, he goes on ahead of them. His sheep follow him because they know his voice.
>
> JOHN 10:3b–4

And what about solids? Put your ear to a table and tap the table. Sound waves travel through solids, too. In fact, because the molecules in solids are closer together than in liquids, sound moves more quickly through a wood table than through water. For the same reason, sound also travels more quickly through water than through air.

How fast sound travels depends on the substance it's traveling through. That's why sound waves can't travel at all through outer space. In space there are no air molecules to pass the waves along.

Sound waves travel more quickly through a solid than air. But how does the speed of sound compare with the speed of light? If you've ever watched a distant flash of

38

lightning and counted the seconds before you heard the boom of thunder, then you know. Comparing the two is like comparing the tortoise and the hare. Light travels a speedy 186,206 *miles* per second, compared to sound's pokey 1,100 *feet* per second. A flash of lightning reaches our eyes nearly one million times faster than its boom reaches our ears!

Sound is all around. It's a way for us to take in our surroundings and communicate with others. It's also a way for God to reveal himself to us. He uses sounds we're familiar with to describe His voice so we can better understand Him.

He tells us that His voice thunders, that it roars like rushing waters, that it's like the sound of a loud trumpet or a huge crowd of people. God's voice is so powerful it created the universe. It can raise the dead. Like thunder, it gets our attention.

God's voice has authority, majesty, and beauty. From these we understand that God himself is powerful, majestic, and beautiful. We're inspired to worship Him. We stand in awe and have a healthy fear of Him, too.

To those who know God, His voice is not only powerful, but also a gentle whisper. And just as we recognize the voices of people we know, we recognize the sound of His voice. But His voice isn't heard with our ears; it's heard with our hearts. When we hear the gentle voice of the One who loves us, our hearts are stirred. We respond with love and draw near to Him.

Shh. Sit quietly and listen. Do you hear His voice within your heart?

Thought to remember:

I can hear God's voice with my heart.

Additional verses:

1 Kings 19:11–13; Job 37:5; 40:9; Psalm 29:3–9; Ezekiel 43:2; Revelation 1:10, 15; 3:20

What are some other fun facts about sound waves?

* They bounce back, just as light waves reflect in mirrors. A reflecting sound wave is called an echo. To discover more about reflecting light waves, turn to "Handpicked by God" on page 31.

* Sound waves interfere with one another, as do light and water waves. Sound waves that are out of step with one another produce soft sounds or no sounds at all. (To discover more about interference, turn to "Catch the Wave" on page 35.)

* Sound waves are slightly different from water and light waves. You've seen how water moves up and down as waves pass through it. Light moves in the same way. But air molecules move forward and back when sound waves travel through them.

Check It Out!

To see the vibrations that sound waves create, you need:
* a small, empty can or jar
* some plastic wrap
* a rubber band
* some salt
* a metal pot
* a wooden spoon

Stretch the plastic wrap tightly over the mouth of the jar. Secure it with a rubber band. Sprinkle salt on the plastic. Set the jar on the table. Now hold the pot next to the jar and beat the bottom of the pot with the wooden spoon. Do you see the salt "dance" on top of the plastic? Sound waves cause the salt to move.

DIG DEEPER!

* sound
* waves
* physics

There's a lot on TV and in movies that we're quite sure could never happen in real life. Main characters in dangerous situations go for days without eating or sleeping. They hardly ever suffer a bruise, get dirty, or tear their clothes. Even after long hikes in drenching rains, not a hair is out of place.

Then there's this scene: A woman with a strong, pure voice sings loudly at a wedding. She reaches a piercing high note and holds it. The crystal glass in front of her shatters.

Fact or fiction?

Believe it or not, the scene with the exploding glass could be true. To understand why, it's helpful to know a couple of fun physics facts.

> What I'm about to tell you is true. Anyone who has faith in me will do what I have been doing. In fact, he will do even greater things.
>
> JOHN 14:12

The first fact is so strange it's almost as hard to believe as the things we see on TV. Just about everything in the universe vibrates, or moves back and forth very quickly. That includes atoms, planets, and you!

Not only do objects vibrate, but they also vibrate at a special rate, or **frequency**—usually many times per second. This rate is different for different objects. That's why forks sound different than soccer balls when dropped on the ground. Each has its own natural frequency.

And that brings us back to the singer and the shattered glass. A crystal glass vibrates at its own natural frequency. When the singer reaches the note that matches the natural frequency of the glass, the sound waves from her voice cause the glass to begin to vibrate. As the singer holds the note, each additional sound wave makes the vibrations of the glass increase in size. This is called **resonance**. In this case the size of the vibrations increases until the glass shatters.

Another way to understand resonance is to think of swinging. You begin with a kick to get the motion going. One, two, three, and you're off the ground floating back, then forward, legs stretched to catch the rhythm of the swing. Then it's back again, legs bent, sweeping higher. Then forward, with hair flapping, stomach tumbling, wind whistling, toes touching treetops. Back and forth you soar, pumping with your legs, pulling with your arms, rising higher and higher till you scrape the sky.

frequency:
(FREE-Kwen-See)

How do you figure out the natural frequency of a glass? Wet your finger and run it around the rim of the glass. The glass will hum a certain note. Now put some water in the glass. How does the sound change?

resonance:
(REH-zuh-nents) comes from the Latin word that means "to resound," or sound again

As long as you pump with your legs and pull with your arms in rhythm with the swing's natural frequency, it's easy to fly into the sky. It takes little effort to stay there. That's resonance.

Here are other awesome examples of resonance:

* In the 1800s a troop of soldiers marched in rhythm across a foot-bridge. By chance, the vibrations of their footsteps matched the natural frequency of the bridge. The vibrations in the bridge grew until it collapsed. That's why troops now break step when they cross bridges.

* In 1940 the wind blew in resonance with a Tacoma, Washington, bridge, causing the bridge to twist back and forth. The vibration increased over several hours until the bridge collapsed. Engineers learned from this; today bridges are designed so this doesn't happen.

Of course, not all the effects of resonance are negative. Resonance is used in musical instruments to increase their sound. It's at work in TVs and radios to produce clear pictures and sound. It's also behind some medical equipment used to detect diseases in our bodies.

And it's at work in you! When you believe in Jesus, you receive His life. You could say that the natural frequency of your spirit becomes the same as His. Resonance takes place because vibrations are "in sync" with each other. In a similar way, when you do things—or "vibrate"—in sync with God, surprising and big things can happen in your life, as well.

The Bible is filled with examples of how God's power has resonated in the lives of those who know Him. Moses parted the Red Sea (see Exodus 14:5–28). The walls of Jericho fell at the sound of trumpets and a shout (see Joshua 6:1–20). David killed Goliath with a stone (see 1 Samuel 17:8–11, 32–50). Peter preached and thousands were saved (see Acts 2:22–38, 41). Philip caught up with a chariot, and an Egyptian was saved (see Acts 8:26–39).

We may not part seas or take down walls, but even a simple sentence spoken to another or small acts of love and kindness are increased in surprising ways. That's because it's God power at work through us, causing us to do things far greater than we could ever do on our own.

No matter how hard we try to do God's work, our own pitiful efforts don't amount to much. But when we stop trying and trust His Spirit to work through us, we vibrate with His powerful energy.

Thought to remember:

God's power can resonate in me.

Additional verses:

John 15:5; 1 Corinthians 6:17; Ephesians 2:10; 3:20–21; James 5:17

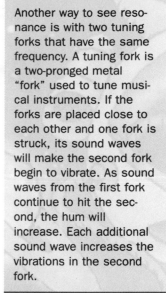

Another way to see resonance is with two tuning forks that have the same frequency. A tuning fork is a two-pronged metal "fork" used to tune musical instruments. If the forks are placed close to each other and one fork is struck, its sound waves will make the second fork begin to vibrate. As sound waves from the first fork continue to hit the second, the hum will increase. Each additional sound wave increases the vibrations in the second fork.

TRY It!

See for yourself how resonance works—go for a swing! How easy is it for you to gain height when you pump your legs in rhythm with the swing? How hard do you have to pump your legs to keep that height once you reach it? Try bending your legs when they should be extended and vice versa. How hard is it to build height when you don't pump in rhythm with the swing?

DIG DEEPER!

* sound
* resonance
* physics

⑮ Irresistible Attraction

Do you know what it means when a person is said to have a magnetic personality? If you've ever played around with magnets, then you probably have a good idea. You know that magnets attract objects such as needles, nails, paper clips—and each other. Of course, people don't attract needles, nails, or paper clips. But they do attract each other. Figuring out why some people draw others to themselves isn't easy. But scientists do have a good idea about why magnets attract objects to themselves. To understand why, let's take a peek inside the atom.

Remember electrons, the tiny particles with negative electrical charges that zip around the center of the atom? While electrons race around the nucleus, they also spin. We know from experiments that a moving electrical charge creates a magnetic field. This means that every spinning electron is an itty-bitty magnet itself! Add bunches of electrons in bunches of atoms together and what do you have? A magnet.

Since all matter in the world is made up of atoms, and they all have spinning electrons, then why aren't we surrounded by magnets? Because electrons also spin in opposite directions. This causes their magnetic fields to cancel one another out. Only metals such as iron, nickel, and cobalt have fields that don't cancel each other out completely. Most of the magnets we use are made of mixtures of these metals.

So how do magnets attract needles, nails, and paper clips? The power of a magnet spreads into the space around it as a magnetic field. If you cover a magnet with a piece of paper and sprinkle iron filings—tiny bits of iron as small as sand—over it, the lines of the magnetic field can be seen. The iron filings concentrate at both ends of the magnet—the north and south poles—where the magnet's power is greatest. The filings form lines that curve from one pole to the other.

A needle, nail, or paper clip brought within a magnetic field finds the magnet **irresistible**. With a snap and a click, they stick to the magnet as if held there by invisible glue. That's because needles, nails, and paper clips have iron inside them. Their atoms line up and become temporary magnets themselves, each with their own north and south poles. Another way to say this is that the objects become **magnetized**. The south pole of a needle is attracted to the north pole of the magnet. And the south pole

> Two north poles repel (ree-PELL), or push away from, each other. So do two south poles. But a north and south pole are drawn together with a snap and a click, because opposites attract.

> irresistible: (ihr-rih-ZIS-tuh-bul) something you can't resist

> magnetize: (MAG-nuh-tize)

> The Lord appeared to us in the past, saying: "I have loved you with an everlasting love; I have drawn you with loving-kindness."
>
> JEREMIAH 31:3
> (NIV)

of a second needle is attracted to the north pole of the first needle. If the magnet is powerful enough, you can make a whole chain of needles . . . or nails . . . or paper clips. Some magnets are so strong that the objects attracted to them are hard to pull away.

Magnets are irresistible to objects with iron in them. In a similar way, God and His love are irresistible to us. What is it about God's love that draws us to Him? Think about His love as you read this story. . . .

Once upon a time there was a frail orphan girl who lived in a village. Pearl wore ragged clothes, and most nights she burrowed into a pile of hay to fall asleep cold and hungry. Every night she fell asleep starved for love.

One day Pearl heard of a kind king who lived in a distant castle. "He takes in useless strays like you," said a villager, spitting. Then pointing to the woods, he laughed. "They say all you have to do is follow that path."

That night Pearl peered at the thick, dark woods from her bed in the hay. *It's too good to be true. But what if there really is such a king?*

Pearl shivered as she abandoned the hay. Once she found the path, the woods seemed gloomy. Pearl stumbled along the rocky trail toward a light gleaming in the distance. When Pearl emerged from the woods, a glorious castle sparkled out of the night.

Cautiously, Pearl stepped forward. A mysterious figure stood at the entrance. Pearl could barely make out the outline of a crown on his head. Then he spoke: "I've been waiting for you, Pearl."

Pearl stopped. Could this be the king—waiting for *me*? "I heard that you take in—" Suddenly drawn to him, Pearl ran into the king's open arms.

He lifted her tenderly. "Welcome home, Pearl." Then, lovingly, the king looked into her eyes. "From now on, I will take care of you. You can call me Daddy."

In many ways we're like Pearl. We have needs that aren't met by others, so we're drawn to God just as needles, nails, and paper clips are drawn to magnets. He accepts us as we are, brings us into His kingdom, makes us His sons and daughters, and takes care of all our needs. He even invites

Here are more magnet facts to attract your attention:

* Even if you cut a magnet in half—or smaller—each piece will still be a magnet, complete with a north and a south pole. Why? Because the moving electrons that give a magnet its power are still there.

* There are many shapes of magnets. They're shaped like bars, horseshoes, Tootsie Rolls, and rings.

* The earth is like a giant magnet. It has magnetic north and south poles. If you dangle a bar-shaped magnet from a string, its north-seeking pole will point toward the south magnetic pole.

* The needle on a compass (KUM-pas) is magnetic. The north-seeking end of the needle always points toward the earth's south magnetic pole (which—as strange as it sounds—is located near the earth's north geographic pole) so you can find your way.

* How can you turn an iron nail into a magnet? By stroking it several times in one direction with a magnet. This causes groups of atoms in the nail to line up in the same direction as the magnet's field.

Check It Out!

Check out what materials are attracted to a magnet. If you don't have a magnet lying around your house, you can buy one at a hobby store. Test the magnet on a variety of objects in your house. Some suggestions: glass, wood, plastic, a plant, dirt, aluminum foil, different types of coins, silverware, and the refrigerator. (*Warning! Don't put the magnet near computers, cassette tapes, or credit cards! A magnet will scramble the information stored on these devices.*)

Dig Deeper!

* magnets
* magnets and electricity

us to freely come to His throne, anytime!

His love is different from anything we could ever find here on earth. Is it any surprise that God's love is irresistible?

Thought to remember:

God's love is irresistible.

Additional verses:

Psalm 63:3; 103:2–4, 8, 11; John 12:32; Ephesians 3:12, 16–19; 1 Thessalonians 1:4; 1 John 3:1

16 Partners

Have you ever noticed that some things just go together? A fork and knife go together. So do needle and thread, honey and bears, a table and chairs. Perhaps when someone sees you, they are quite likely to see your best friend, too!

In the world of science, we also find two more partners: electricity and magnetism.

In 1820 a Danish scientist named Hans Christian **Oersted** discovered just how electricity and magnetism go together. Oersted discovered a simple secret. When he placed a compass near a wire with electricity going through it, the compass needle no longer pointed north. The needle now pointed toward the wire! Oersted saw the partnership between electricity and magnetism and called it electromagnetism. A wire with an electric current—a flow of electrical charges—running through it is always surrounded by a magnetic field.

Can we also flip-flop this friendship between electricity and magnetism? Can a magnet produce electricity? Yes! In 1831 an Englishman named Michael **Faraday** and an American man named Joseph Henry learned that when a magnet is moved in and out of a coil of wire, an electrical current is produced in the wire. The key to the discovery was that the magnet had to be moving. Simply placing the magnet inside the wire did nothing.

These simple secrets—brought to light in 1820 and 1831—were giant discoveries. Without an understanding of this relationship, we wouldn't have electricity at our fingertips. The electricity that flows into our homes, schools, and stores begins in **generators** at power plants. Generators are coils of wire that **rotate** inside large magnets to produce, or generate, electricity. The link between electricity and magnetism is also behind all the electric motors that we take advantage of, from hair dryers to refrigerators to electric screwdrivers.

In the world of science, electrical currents and magnetism go together. As we journey through this world with God, we also discover two more best friends: faith and good works.

When we come to God by believing in Jesus—or by faith—we get to share in the riches of His life. But that's not all. Coming to God by faith also means that we get to

> Oersted:
> (UR-sted)
>
> To discover more about the relationship between electricity and magnetism, turn to "Invisible Energy" on page 16.

To discover more about the relationship between electricity and magnetism, turn to "Invisible Energy" on page 16.

> Faraday:
> (FARE-uh-day)
>
> To produce a stronger current, you can use more loops of wire, move the magnet or wire more quickly, or use a stronger magnet.

> generator:
> (JEN-er-ay-ter)

> rotate:
> (ROW-tate)
> to spin

> The only thing that really counts is faith that shows itself through love.
>
> GALATIANS 5:6b

Oersted was doing a demonstration in front of a class to prove there was no partnership between electricity and magnetism when he discovered there really was one. You can imagine how surprised he was at the results!

Faraday was the son of a blacksmith. Although he had little education, he did have an inventive mind and a thirst to learn. Along with his discovery that magnets could produce an electric field, he's also known for important findings in chemistry and for inventing the first electric motor.

Make It!

To make an electromagnet, you need

* about two feet of insulated wire with the insulation stripped off each end

* a large iron nail

* a 9-volt battery

* paper clips or iron shavings

Coil the wire tightly around the nail. Hook each end of the wire around a battery terminal. You now have an electromagnet! The nail will pick up the paper clips and iron shavings.

DIG DEEPER!

* electromagnetism
* electricity
* magnetism

share in the work He's doing in other people's lives. That's exciting!

When the Spirit of God brings people who have needs across our paths, and we're in a position to help them, what should we do? Ignore them, tell them we'll pray for them, or help them out? The Spirit of God who lives inside us cares about others, and He does it in a practical way. It just so happens that we are His tools; He chooses to work through us.

Sometimes giving a helping hand to others is hard. It can mean giving up something we'd rather hold on to. But these kinds of good works show that our faith in Jesus is real, because without real faith, we couldn't do them.

True faith in Jesus produces good works. Faith and good works belong together, like electricity and magnetism, a fork and knife, needle and thread, honey and bears, a table and chairs. . . .

Thought to remember:

Faith in Jesus produces good works in our lives.

Additional verses:

Matthew 5:16; 1 Corinthians 15:10; 2 Corinthians 5:20a; 9:7–8; Ephesians 2:8–10; James 2:15–17, 26

Try this multiple-choice question just for fun:

a. Electricity comes from electrons.

b. Electricity comes from atoms.

c. Electricity comes from the power plant.

d. There are basically two forms of electricity.

e. All of the above.

If you said a, b, c, or d is true, give yourself a hand. If you said all of these statements about electricity are true, give yourself a standing ovation. Let's take a closer look.

As you learned before, atoms have tiny particles with electrical charges. Protons, in the center of atoms, have positive charges. Electrons, which whirl around outside the center, have negative charges. Normally there are the same number of protons and electrons in each atom, so they balance each other out. Atoms with an equal number of protons and electrons have no overall charge.

Sometimes atoms lose or gain some of their outer electrons. Have you ever gotten a charge out of rubbing a balloon against your clothing so it would stick to you? The friction causes your clothing to lose electrons to the balloon. Now your clothing has more protons than electrons; it becomes positively charged. And the balloon? The extra electrons give it a negative charge. Since positive and negative charges attract each other, the balloon sticks to you. It's positively amazing!

> I DIDN'T PREACH MY MESSAGE WITH CLEVER AND COMPELLING WORDS. AS I PREACHED, THE HOLY SPIRIT SHOWED HIS POWER. THAT WAS SO YOU WOULD BELIEVE NOT BECAUSE OF HUMAN WISDOM BUT BECAUSE OF GOD'S POWER.
>
> 1 CORINTHIANS 2:4–5

static: (STAT-ik)

To discover more about a shocking display of static electricity—lightning—turn to "Thunder Power" on page 75.

This kind of electricity is called **static** electricity. To remember it, think of electricity that rests. The word *static* means to stay in one place, or to rest. Static electricity results from charges that rest on objects.

Static electricity doesn't run lights, refrigerators, or radios, though. To operate TVs, toasters, and telephones, we need electrical charges to move. Electricity on the move is called current electricity; the word *current* comes from a word that means *to run*.

Here are more positively electric facts about conductors:

* Aluminum is another great conductor of electricity.

* Water also conducts electricity. Adding salt helps electricity to flow even better.

* Metals are also good conductors of heat.

* Some electrical energy is lost as it travels through copper wire. Certain metals, called superconductors, allow electricity to flow through them without losing much energy at all. These metals only behave as superconductors at super low temperatures, but researchers are working to produce materials that are superconductors at warmer temperatures.

Turning a wire coil inside a magnet creates electrical energy at a power plant. The electricity then moves, or flows, from its source to our houses.

To get to our houses, current electricity needs a material to flow through. It travels through wires, usually copper wires. Why? Because copper is a metal, and metals are good **conductors** of electricity. The atoms in metals don't hold on tightly to their outer electrons. These loosely held, or "free," electrons form a cloud of electrons that electrical energy can easily flow through. As current is produced at the power plant, it's passed from electron to electron to your home at nearly the speed of light.

If you tried to run an electrical current through wood, glass, rubber, or plastic, you'd find they flunk the test for conducting current. Why? Atoms that make up these materials hold on tightly to their electrons. Their electrons aren't as free to wander as they are in metals. Materials that are stubborn when it comes to conducting electricity are called **insulators**. We use insulators to surround wire. They keep us from getting shocked.

Conductors made of metal bring electricity into our homes and schools so we can benefit from conveniences such as computers, CD players, and VCRs. God uses a different kind of conductor to carry the power of His life into this world. What does He use to conduct His life? The "what" is a "who," and it can be you!

While God visited the earth as Jesus, His power was clear to many who came in contact with Him. But then Jesus returned to heaven. Was God's influence on earth gone? No. He uses people as conductors. His power flows through those who follow Him to touch the lives of others.

The wires that carry electrical current don't create the current; their job is to just let it flow. The power plant is the source of the electrical power. In a similar way, we don't have to try to figure out ways to come up with the current of God's love on our own; our job is to just let it flow. Only God can be the source of His powerful love.

As we depend on God and listen to His urgings with a ready heart, we will see Him work in the lives of those

CONDUCTOR: (KuN-DUCK-teR) a material that allows electricity to flow through it

INSULATOR: (IN-SuH-Lay-teR)

we come in contact with. We will see His power bring light into our own lives and the lives of others. It's amazing that God would use us to conduct the current of His love to this world. It's electrifying!

Thought to remember:

I can be a conductor of God's power!

Additional verses:

John 15:4–5; Acts 1:8; Romans 15:13 (NIV);
2 Corinthians 4:6–7; Ephesians 3:20;
2 Timothy 1:7 (NIV)

DiSCoVeR It!

Discover which materials are conductors and insulators. To do this activity, use the electric circuit with battery and light bulb described in "Flip the Switch" on page 50. You will also need a small piece of paper, aluminum foil, a plastic bag, a Popsicle stick, a pair of glasses, a plant leaf, and any kind of fabric.

Stick each of the above materials between the knobby end of the battery and the light bulb. Which of these materials conducts electricity and allows the light bulb to glow? Which materials act as insulators, stopping the flow of electricity?

DIG DEEPER!

★ electricity
★ conductors, insulators
★ metals

18 Flip the Switch

Have you ever stopped to think about the amount of

power we have at our fingertips? All it takes is the flip of a switch to make a light bulb glow, or the push of a button to watch a TV show. Just a light touch of our fingers allows electrical energy to flow into all kinds of appliances that make us comfortable and let us live like kings.

How does an electrical switch work?

To understand, let's pretend that we're the electrical energy. Let's start back at the power plant and travel to a home and into a light bulb. To make the trip, we'll need a path or a road, won't we? That pathway is made of wires, and it's called a **circuit**. For us to make the round trip from the power plant to a home and then back to the power plant without stopping, there can't be any breaks or gaps along the circuit. A gap in a circuit is like a break in the road. There's no way to drive across! But if there are no gaps—or the circuit is complete—we will flow right into a house and straight into a light bulb to heat it up and make it glow.

We all know that our lights aren't on all the time. So what happens to turn them off? That's where the switch comes in. Can you guess how a switch would stop electrical energy from flowing? If you're puzzled, think about the circuit. A broken circuit doesn't allow the energy to pass through. The switch creates a gap in the circuit. It opens the circuit so we can't complete the journey to the light bulb.

Inside the switch are two small metal buttons called *contacts*. To turn off a light bulb, a person flips the switch. The contacts are pushed apart, a gap is created, and the flow of electricity is stopped. What happens when a person flips the switch the opposite way to turn on the light bulb? The contacts are brought together again. The circuit is complete. Like a bridge across the broken road, a pathway is created that allows us to make it all the way to the light bulb, and the world becomes a brighter place. Simple, isn't it!

When it comes to our spiritual lives, you could say there's a switch in our hearts. Jesus tells us to continue, or remain, in Him. He wants us to enjoy His companion-

circuit: (SIR-kit)

APPliances are plugged into outlets. They have built-in switches that we turn on and off with touch pads, knobs, and dials.

> Here I am! I stand at the door and knock. If any of you hears my voice and opens the door, I will come in and eat with you. And you will eat with me.
>
> REVELATION 3:20

ship, to keep company or have fellowship with Him every moment of every day.

But sometimes we flip the switch to our hearts and break the circuit that lets His life light up our lives. That happens when we insist on doing things our own way and in our own strength. God calls this walking in the "flesh." It's the opposite of walking in the power of the Spirit.

How do people behave when the switch to their hearts is flipped to the "off" position? Here are a few examples: We might lie or refuse to take responsibility when we mess up. We might be jealous, brag about ourselves, or want to get back at others. Perhaps we're pushy or demand our own way. Being grouchy, complaining, and feeling sorry for ourselves are also signs of the flesh.

Walking in the flesh is no way to live! We're miserable when we act this way, and we make everyone around us miserable, too. So what do we do when we realize we're not keeping company with Jesus? All it takes is a flip of the switch to our hearts to close the gap that completes the circuit. We do this when we say, "I'm sorry, God! I've messed up. I can't do anything without you." God is always ready to flow through us. Jesus is always waiting for us to close the gap and walk with Him.

Thought to remember:

I want to keep the "switch" of my heart turned on to Jesus.

Additional verses:

Psalm 66:18; 84:2, 10; John 15:4; Galatians 5:19–25 (NIV); 1 John 1:9

Buildings today have safety features that automatically switch off electricity if necessary. One is a circuit breaker. Its name tells you what it does. It breaks, or trips, the circuit to stop the flow of electricity. Circuit breakers trip when too many appliances are used at one time and electrical wires begin to heat up. Circuit breakers prevent fires.

Another special device is the ground fault circuit interrupter, or GFCI for short. You've probably seen them in your bathroom or anywhere there's an outlet near water. GFCIs sense when electrical current is going where it shouldn't—into you—and instantly shut it off. These plugs can keep you from getting shocked. GFCIs save lives, but remember—even when using a GFCI plug, it's very dangerous to operate electrical appliances near bathtubs or over water in sinks.

Make It!

To make a circuit, you need a size D battery, two wire twist ties, tape, and a flashlight bulb.

Peel the plastic off the ends of the wires to expose the metal. Twist two ends together to make one strand of wire. Tape one end of the wire to the flat disc (the negative end) of the battery. Wrap the other end of the wire around the metal base of the flashlight bulb.

Now touch the bottom of the light bulb to the knob that sticks out at the other end of the battery. The bulb should light up. When you separate the base of the bulb from the battery, there's a gap. The circuit is broken and the light turns off. In a similar way, a light switch creates a gap to turn off lights.

DIG DEEPER!

* electricity
* electrical circuits
* switches

Can you imagine life without electricity?

There's no doubt about it—we enjoy our lights, boom boxes, and electronic toys. But what do we do when we want to roam away from home, when we're not near electrical outlets?

Whether by foot, plane, or car . . . no matter how near and no matter how far, we need portable power that we can place in our packs, pockets, or purses. What is the source of power that we use anywhere, anytime, or anyplace? Batteries. Power to go.

They come in many shapes and sizes—from round button batteries smaller than thumbtacks to box-shaped batteries large enough to power submarines. No matter what they look like, though, all batteries have two things in common. Batteries have two different chemicals, with either a liquid or paste in between them. The electrical current comes from chemical reactions inside the batteries.

To understand the way a battery is put together and how it works, picture a tube-shaped battery, such as the kind you put in flashlights. If you split the battery lengthwise down the middle, you would see that it has layers. On the outside is a thin zinc case. Inside this is a thick, pasty substance. And at the very core is a rod made of carbon that looks sort of like a nail.

The zinc case and carbon core are both called **electrodes**. They produce the positive and negative electrical charges that make electricity flow when we turn on our toys. The pasty substance in the middle is an **electrolyte**. It conducts the electrical charge from one electrode to another. The electrolyte makes it possible for chemical reactions to happen at the electrodes.

One chemical reaction causes electrons to flow from the zinc case to the flat, or negative, end of the battery, then through the toy that needs power to run. Another chemical reaction inside the battery gives a positive charge to the end of the battery with the little bump that sticks out. This attracts the negative electrical charge moving through the toy. As the charge moves through the toy, it gives the toy the energy needed to move or light up.

Batteries are great because they are portable pocket power. But there's one problem

---

Do not actually cut open a battery! Batteries contain chemicals that can hurt you.

electrode:
(ee-ZEK-trode)

electrolyte:
(ee-ZEK-truh-Lite)

There's a fancy way to say God is all-powerful. He's omnipotent (om-NIH-puh-tent).

WISDOM AND POWER BELONG TO GOD. ADVICE AND UNDERSTANDING ALSO BELONG TO HIM. STRENGTH AND SUCCESS BELONG TO HIM.

JOB 12:13, 16a

with batteries. As a source of power, they're limited. The chemicals inside batteries get used up. Their power runs dry. In spite of what commercials want you to believe, the Energizer Bunny will not keep on going forever.

In a way, we are like batteries. In and of ourselves, we have limited power to help others or ourselves. We have limited love, limited strength, and limited wisdom and understanding. That becomes clear when we face problems that are too hard for us—or anybody else—to solve. It's when the going gets rough and our power dries up that we find out we can't keep going and going and going. We discover that we need a more perfect power. That power is found in God. When we first put our trust in Jesus, we become "plugged in" to a source of power far, far greater than our own. In fact, His power is greater than great. It's without limit, because He's without limits. We can go to God to draw upon His power, knowing that He is everything we need for a new life and to keep on going.

Instead of depending on our own or someone else's pocket power, why not go directly to the perfect source of unlimited power?

Thought to remember:
God has unlimited power. I can go to Him.

Additional verses:
Psalm 33:16–22; 146:3–6; 147:5, 10–11; Romans 11:33–36 (NIV); Philippians 4:19

Raise your battery IQ. Here's another batch of battery facts!

★ Batteries with pasty electrolytes are called dry-cell batteries. Some batteries, such as the ones in cars, have liquid electrolytes. They're called wet-cell batteries.

★ Batteries that quit working when their chemicals are used up are called primary (PRY-mary) batteries. Some batteries can be recharged after they run out of energy, though. These are called secondary (SECK-und-air-ee) batteries.

★ Plugging secondary batteries into an electrical outlet recharges them. The current reverses the chemical reactions, making more of the chemicals needed so the battery can produce electricity again.

Make It!

Make a lemon battery! You will need

★ a lemon (works as the electrolyte)

★ a two- to three-inch strand of copper wire (works as an electrode)

★ a paper clip, unwound and cut into a two- to three-inch piece (works as an electrode)

Roll the lemon against a counter to make it squishy. Poke the copper wire into the lemon. Poke the piece of paper clip into the lemon close to the copper wire, but don't let them touch. Touch the loose ends of both wires to the tip of your tongue. (Hint: Extra spit on the end of your tongue helps!) Do you feel a tiny tingle? Is there a slight metallic taste?

Is a lemon battery a wet- or dry-cell battery? Why? The answer is on page 149.

DIG DEEPER!
★ batteries
★ electricity

20 Measuring Up

Suppose you're building a doghouse for Tiny, your Great
Dane. The blueprints call for six pieces of wood; each needs to be four carrots
long. Raiding the refrigerator, you pull out a few carrots. Hmm. Slight problem
here. All these carrots are different lengths. Should you use a long carrot or a short
one?

None of us would think of measuring with a carrot, would we? But believe it or
not, at one time people used all sorts of things to measure length and weight. Seeds
and stones were used to measure weight. Arms,
hands, feet, and fingers were used as guidelines to
measure length.

As you can imagine, people had the same problem
with seeds, stones, and body parts that you had with
carrots! None of these give consistent measurements. How did people solve this problem?

They came up with a standard, a model to base all
their measurements on. At first, a king's foot, arm,
hand, and fingers became the guidelines for length.
Eventually, though, a better system of measurement
was invented. In the late 1700s the French developed a uniform method for measuring amounts.
This grew into the modern **metric** system now used
by nearly everyone around the world. Length is
measured in meters; weight is measured in newtons.
Today these are part of the International System of
Units—abbreviated SI—that doesn't change. The SI
also includes standards for time, temperature, electrical current, and the brightness of light.

metric:
(MEH-trik) comes
from the Greek
word "metron,"
which means
"measure"

> Everyone has sinned. No
> one measures up to
> God's glory. The free
> gift of God's grace
> makes all of us right
> with Him. Christ Jesus
> paid the price to set us
> free. God gave Him as a
> sacrifice to pay for
> sins. So He forgives the
> sins of those who have
> faith in His blood.
>
> ROMANS 3:23–25a

Even though the metric system is used around the world, most people in the
United States still don't use it for everyday measurements. Instead, pounds are used
to figure out how much something weighs. Inches measure length. Inches are based
on an old Roman system. The width of one thumb is about one inch. Twelve thumbs
fit into the length of a human's foot, and three feet fit in one yard.

The inch-pound system is the everyday standard in the United States, but

American scientists use the metric system. Can you figure out why? One reason is scientists work a lot with numbers and quantities. If scientists from the United States used the inch-pound system, scientists from the rest of the world wouldn't understand a thing they were talking about! Using the same standard gets rid of confusion. Plus, the metric system is easier to use.

Just as there is one standard that scientists use for measuring our physical world, God has one standard for our lives, as well. Do you have some ideas about what that standard could be?

Is it being good? Being nice? Being honest all the time? Being faithful about going to church?

These are all good things, but they aren't God's standard for us. God's standard is Jesus.

Having Jesus as our standard can seem scary! Deep down in our hearts, all of us know that even our best efforts could never measure up to Jesus. He is perfect all the time.

Not living up to God's standard makes us His enemies. So what's the answer?

The answer is to stop trying to reach the standard by our own efforts. Instead, believe in Jesus. God is kind to us. He knew we could never be perfect like Jesus. That's why He makes us able to measure up to the standard by giving us Jesus' perfect life.

It's amazing and exciting that God gave us a standard and then put the standard inside us so we can live it. What a relief!

Thought to remember:
Jesus lives up to God's standard for me.

Additional verses:
Isaiah 64:6; Ezekiel 36:26–27 (NIV); Colossians 1:21–22; 2 Timothy 1:9

Long ago in Egypt, the arm and fingers were used to measure length.

* The distance from the elbow to the tip of the middle finger is called a **cubit** (Q-bit).

* The width of a stretched-out hand from the thumb to little finger is called a span.

* The width of one finger is called a digit (DIH-jit).

* The width of four fingers is called a palm.

DISCOVER It!
Discover for yourself how the old-fashioned way of measuring causes confusion. Grab a friend, a ruler, a pencil, and a piece of paper. Make two columns. Put your name at the top of one column and your friend's name at the top of the other. Record the following measurements for your friend and yourself. Measure

* the width of your thumb with the ruler. How many thumb widths fit in the length of your foot? How does your foot compare to the twelve inches of a ruler?

* the width of four fingers.

* the width of your stretched-out hand, from little finger to thumb.

* the distance from the elbow to the tip of the middle finger.

How do your measurements compare? Why is it important to use a standard unit of measurement?

DIG DEEPER!
* measurement, measuring

* metric system

* the International System of Units

Have you ever noticed that we live in a mixed-up world?

Button up your lab coat, make sure your safety glasses are snug, and grab a microscope. It's time to explore the world of mixtures.

Let's begin by taking a seat at a table filled with party foods. Mmm. Hope you're hungry! As you can see, we've got pepperoni pizza with mushrooms and olives here, tuna-noodle casserole over there. Also lasagna, lemon Jell-O, and tossed salad with oil-and-vinegar dressing. For dessert you have a choice of chocolate-chip ice cream, oatmeal raisin cookies, and blueberry muffins. And to wash it all down, we have milk, water, tea sweetened with sugar, and a punch made from powdered mix.

By now you might be wondering what a pizza party has to do with science. Chemists like to organize materials into groups that share common qualities. This helps them understand why materials behave the way they do. The foods on our table—and many other substances in our world—are *mixtures*. In a mixture, two or more materials are combined, but each material keeps its own qualities. Substances in mixtures can be separated from each other pretty easily.

In many cases, you can easily tell apart the different materials that make up mixtures. These mixtures are not the same, or uniform, all the way

Heterogeneous:
(Het-er-oh-JEE-nee-us)

through. They're called **heterogeneous** mixtures. Our party pizza is made of several distinct parts that you could sort: pepperoni, cheese, crust, sauce, olives, and mushrooms.

Now reread the list of treats on our table and decide which foods are heterogeneous. Did you list tuna-noodle casserole, lasagna, tossed salad, oil-and-vinegar dressing, chocolate-chip ice cream, oatmeal raisin cookies, and blueberry muffins? What about milk?

> I have become all things to all people so that in all possible ways I might save some.
>
> 1 CORINTHIANS 9:22b
>
> Dear friends, you are outsiders and strangers in this world. So I'm asking you not to give in to your sinful longings. . . . People who don't believe might say you are doing wrong. But lead good lives among them. Then they will see your good works.
>
> 1 PETER 2:11–12a

Most of the milk we buy at the store is labeled "homogenized," but it's really a hetero-geneous mixture "pretending" to be homogeneous. The fat globules in milk are broken up into very small particles so that they're mixed evenly throughout.

Homogeneous: (HO-MO-JEE-nee-us)

Homogeneous mixtures are also called solutions. Many solutions are liquid, but some are gases and solids. Air is a solution made of gases. Brass is a metal solution made of a mixture of the metals copper and zinc.

Gentile: (JEN-tile) Someone who isn't Jewish

It's a bit tricky. Milk looks as if it's the same throughout, but if you whip out your microscope, you'll see tiny globs of fat that are distinct from the rest of the liquid. So milk is heterogeneous, too. The fat globules in milk are broken up into very small particles so that they're distributed evenly throughout.

What about foods that don't fit into the heterogeneous group? These mixtures are the same, or uniform, all the way through. They're called **homogeneous**. What items on our table are homogeneous? Jello-O is. So is water, sweetened tea, and the punch made from powdered mix. If you inspect one part of Jell-O, water, tea, or punch, each part will be like every other part.

Did you know that, as we live our lives in this world, we can be homogeneous or heterogeneous? When we mix with others, we can blend in or be distinct. How do you think God wants us to live our lives on this earth?

In the New Testament Paul said that he became like other people so they might know Jesus. In a way, he was homogeneous. To Jews, Paul became like a Jew. To **Gentiles**, he became like a Gentile. To the weak, he became weak. As Paul mixed and fit in with people who were different from him, he got to know them. They trusted him.

But even though Paul fit in with those who didn't know Jesus, his life was distinct. He didn't take part in the sins of those who didn't know Jesus. With Jesus' life inside, he could love as Jesus loves. Because Paul's life was different from those around him who didn't know Jesus, he was also heterogeneous. People could see that Jesus made a difference in His life.

We are like Paul, too.

When we come to Jesus, He gives us His life. We have a different way of living and looking at the world. We become foreigners while still living in the world. So even though we mix with others and become close to them, the power of Jesus' life in us also makes us distinct. This attracts others who are searching for Jesus.

Heterogeneous? Or homogeneous? As we mix with this world, we're both.

There are many homogeneous materials that aren't mixtures.

Elements such as gold, iron, silver, and oxygen are homogeneous substances because they're the same throughout. But elements aren't mixtures.

When the atoms of one element join with the atoms of a different element, a new substance called a **compound** (KOM-pound) forms. Salt is made up of two certain elements that have joined together. Salt is a homogeneous material, but it's not a mixture. Separating the substances in compounds is harder than separating the materials that make up mixtures.

Make It!

To make your own hetero-geneous and homogeneous mixtures, all you need are two glasses, milk, chocolate powder or syrup, and food coloring.

Pour milk into one of the glasses. Stir in some chocolate powder or syrup. Let the mixture sit for an hour. Some of the chocolate will settle to the bottom of the glass. This mixture is heterogeneous.

Now pour water into the second glass. Add food coloring and stir. This mixture is the same all the way through. It's homogeneous.

Explore It!

Below is a list of mixtures. If you think the substance is a heterogeneous mixture, put a 1 next to it. If you think the substance is a homogeneous mixture, write a 2 next to it.

air:

smoggy air:

sandstone:

soil:

food coloring dissolved in water:

salt water:

window glass:

house paint:

water with ice cubes:

sand:

coffee:

a brick:

concrete:

wood:

The answers are on page 149.

DIG DEEPER!

★ chemistry
★ mixtures
★ matter

Thought to remember:

As I mix with the world, I am heterogeneous and homogeneous.

Additional verses:

John 13:34; 1 Corinthians 9:19–23; 2 Corinthians 6:14–18; 1 Peter 1:1; 2:9–12

⚫22 From the Inside Out

Might as well get it over with, Annie thinks, peeking at the snowstorm through icy windows. Snuggling into a puffy jacket, she stuffs her hands into gloves, her feet into boots. She lifts the heavy ax from hooks in the garage. With a shiver Annie steps into the cold, turning her face away from the whipping snow.

Annie rests the ax against a tree and balances the end of a pine log on top of a wide stump. Sucking in a big breath, Annie raises the ax above her head. Her concentration shifts from the heavy ax to the log. With a huff that sends out a cloud of white breath, she brings down the ax. *Chunk.* The sharp edge of the ax bites into the log. Shaking the axhead free, Annie once more balances the log and raises the ax. *Chunk.* Splinters fly. The gash deepens. Another swing, and the wood splits in two.

> Anyone who believes in Christ is a new creation. The old is gone! The new has come! It is all from God.
>
> 2 CORINTHIANS 5:17–18a

An armload of wood later, Annie holds a burning match to loose wads of newspaper, over which she's built a tepee of small logs. *Whoosh.* The hot tongues of flame curl around the wood. Steam rises from the pine, and then, with a snap and a pop, the logs catch on fire. As Annie warms her hands, snow melts from her hair and drips to the floor.

State: the condition or form of a substance. Ice is the solid state of water. Steam is the gaseous state of water.

In this description of splitting wood and building a fire, you may have noticed that changes to wood and water take place. In our physical world, many materials go through changes. Some of these are physical changes. This means the substance is still the same after the physical change has taken place.

In this example, although wood is cut, split, and splintered, it's still wood. And in this example, ice, snow, steam, dripping water, and Annie's cloudy breath are all different forms, or **states**, of one substance: water. Only physical changes have taken place.

chemical: (KEM-ih-kul)

But what happens when wood is burned? Is that a physical change? When wood—or any substance—burns, a new substance with new qualities forms. It's no longer the same substance, because a **chemical** change has taken place. The way atoms and mol-

What are some other examples of physical and chemical changes?

* We can pound iron into a different shape, and it will still be iron. But if we expose iron to water and air, the iron rusts. This is a chemical change.

* Sugar dissolves in water, but the two substances don't react with each other. Dissolving is only a physical change. The water can be boiled off and the sugar will remain. On the other hand, heating sugar by itself produces a chemical change that makes black carbon.

* If you combine the poisonous yellow-green gas **chlorine** (KLORE-een) with the silvery metal **sodium** (SO-dee-um), what do you get? A completely new substance: table salt. Salt is the result of a chemical reaction between chlorine and sodium.

Make It!

See physical and chemical changes firsthand!

To see a physical change, you need a piece of paper and a bowl of water. Wad the paper into a ball or cut it into pieces small enough to fit in the bowl. What happens to the paper as it absorbs water? It becomes soggy, doesn't it? But is the paper still paper? Yes! All you've done is change the paper physically.

To see a chemical change, you need a bowl, baking soda, and vinegar (found in the kitchen cupboard. Ask permission first!). Sprinkle some baking soda into the bowl. Set the bowl in a sink. Now pour vinegar over the baking soda. What happens? The substance bubbles and rises. The combination of vinegar and baking soda produces three new substances, including a gas called **carbon dioxide** (CAR-bun die-OX-ide).

DIG DEEPER!

* matter
* physical and chemical changes
* chemistry

ecules are arranged in the new substance is different from the way they were arranged before.

Did you know that something similar to physical and chemical changes can take place in our lives, too?

If you cut your hair, change your style of clothes, or trade glasses for contacts, your outward appearance would be different, wouldn't it? People might not even recognize you.

Or if you pick new friends, act polite instead of rude, pray every day, and start going to church, your outward behavior would be changed. You might seem like a different person.

If you look different on the outside or your behavior changes, are you a new person? No! Like the physical changes that take place when wood is split into logs, you might look or act differently, but you'd still be the same person as before. You remain the same on the inside, in your heart.

How can you change on the inside? When you believe in Jesus, He gives you His life and puts a completely new heart in you. This isn't a heart that pumps your blood. It's the part of you that responds to God. In a way, this is like a chemical reaction, because Jesus plus you makes a totally new you. The old you is gone; a new you is formed. Your new life can look much different on the outside, too, because Jesus' life can now shine through you. He makes you different from the inside out.

Thought to remember:

Jesus makes me totally new!

Additional verses:

Ezekiel 36:26; John 1:12–13; 3:3; 1 Corinthians 2:16b; Galatians 2:20; 2 Peter 1:3–4

A One-Act Play

CHARACTERS:

Freddie Fuddlehead, *seven years old, alleged victim of a theft*
Detective Bungle
Detective Knowall

(Freddie Fuddlehead stands at his round kitchen table. Next to him is Detective Bungle, training a magnifying glass on a tall glass of iced tea. Detective Knowall pulls on latex gloves, opens and closes cabinets.)

Detective Bungle: *(Ready with pen and notebook.)* Tell me exactly what happened, Freddie.

Freddie: It was hot this afternoon. I came inside, poured myself a glass of iced tea, added two spoons of sugar, and stirred. The next thing I knew—right there in the glass—the sugar just disappeared!

Detective Bungle: Did you see anyone nearby?

Freddie: Just my mother. She walked upstairs, carrying my baby sister.

Detective Bungle: Little sister, huh? We'd better fingerprint—

Detective Knowall: *(Picks up glass, holds it up to the light, takes a sip.)* I have the solution. Actually, the solution is a solution. Bring me a spoon!

(Freddie hurries to the drawer for a spoon. He hands it to Detective Knowall, who spoons sugar into the tea. Detective Bungle steps back, crossing his arms.)

Detective Knowall: See what happens when I add more sugar and stir? *(Freddie leans forward. His eyes get big.)* The sugar disappears, all right. But it's obvious that the sugar only *appears* to disappear. Let me explain. *(Adjusts his glasses and pushes up his sleeves.)* What you have here is

> I can do everything by the power of Christ. He gives me strength.
>
> PHILIPPIANS 4:13

Here are more fun facts about solutions:

* The substance that does the dissolving is called a **solvent** (SALL-vent). In "The Case of the Disappearing Sugar," the water in the iced tea is the solvent.

* The substance that dissolves in the solvent is called a **solute** (SALL-yute). In this story, sugar is the solute. There's usually less solute than solvent.

* Gases can dissolve in liquids, as in the case of the gas bubbles in pop.

* Liquids can dissolve in liquids, as in the case of vinegar. Vinegar is water mixed with another liquid, **acetic** (uh-SEE-tik) acid.

* Liquids can dissolve in gases, as in the case of water in air.

a **solution** of sugar and iced tea. If you recall a bit of basic chemistry, sugar crystals are made up of molecules. These molecules have an electrical charge. But so do the water molecules in the tea. The molecules of sugar and water are attracted to each other. So the water molecules surround the sugar crystals, the molecules that make up the sugar break apart from each other, and (*Wiggles his fingers.*) floating away, they mix in with the rest of the solution. In other words, the sugar **dissolves**. Have a taste. (*Hands the glass to Freddie.*)

Freddie: Mmm. Sweet. So the sugar is still here—it's just dissolved in the iced tea?

Detective Knowall: Right-o. (*Grabs the glass and pours in a lot more sugar. Detective Bungle places hands on hips, taps his foot.*) Now, if I add even more sugar to the tea, I have to stir it even more to get it to dissolve. Finally, the tea reaches a point where it can hold no more sugar. The solution is **saturated**. No more sugar will dissolve. (*Holds up his pointer finger and winks.*) But I have a trick. Freddie, heat this in the microwave.

Freddie: (*Starts microwave.*) What does warming the tea have to do with dissolving sugar? (*Microwave dings. Gingerly, Freddie returns it to the table.*)

Detective Knowall: Stir in more sugar, Freddie.

Freddie: It's dissoving! Increasing the temperature lets the tea hold more sugar.

Detective Knowall: Right-o. Now when the solution cools, it's more than saturated, it's *super*saturated.

Freddie: (*Takes a taste, squinches his eyes, and sticks out his tongue.*) Ew. Now it's way too sweet.

Detective Knowall: The case of the missing sugar is solved.

Detective Bungle: (*Scratches his head.*) I'll get the fingerprint kit.

SOLUTION: a mixture that's the same all the way through. Solutions are homogeneous mixtures. To discover more about homogeneous mixtures, turn to "The Big Mix-Up" on page 56.

DISSOLVE: (DIH-ZOLV)

SATURATE: (SATCH-uh-rate)

Raising the temperature doesn't always have a big effect on how well a substance dissolves. The amount of table salt that dissolves in water changes very little when the temperature is raised.

Do you ever feel as if you're saturated—you've had enough and can't possibly take any more? Of course, there may have been times when you ate too much candy, and you know that another bite of sugar will make you sick! But we're talking about a different kind of saturation here.

Perhaps you've had all you can take of an enemy—or even an annoying friend. You understand that Jesus says that we're to love those who are hard to love. But you've tried your best, and now you've had it. You're saturated. All you can think about is getting even or getting away.

Believe it or not, sometimes the people who bother us most are the ones who are best for us. Why? Because they show us something about ourselves. Our struggles with others show us that we can't love in the unselfish way that Jesus does.

So what's the solution? Jesus is the solution. When we understand that we can't love the way He does, we can turn to Him with our willing hearts, and He'll love others through us.

God gave us commands that are impossible for us to carry out in our own strength. But that's why—along with His commands—He gave us Jesus. Depending on Jesus is the secret to *super*saturated love.

Thought to remember:

Jesus is the solution. He'll love others through me.

Additional verses:

Matthew 5:43–44; 1 Corinthians 13:4–8; 2 Corinthians 12:9; Galatians 5:14; 2 Timothy 1:7 (NIV); 1 John 5:3–5

Explore It!

See for yourself how sugar dissolves in water. Pour about a cup of water into a clear glass. Add a teaspoon of sugar and stir. Does the sugar dissolve? How can you tell?

Continue to add sugar, a teaspoon at a time, keeping track of how many spoonfuls you're adding. How many teaspoons does it take before the sugar stops dissolving? The solution is now saturated.

With permission from your parents, pour the mixture into a pot and heat it until it begins to boil. Now how much more sugar can you add before the sugar stops dissolving? Once it cools, this solution will be supersaturated.

Dig Deeper!

* chemistry
* solutions
* mixtures
* matter

Oil and Water Don't Mix

Have you ever heard the saying "Oil and water don't mix"? If you've ever added oil to water, then you know it's true. At first globs of oil float around in the water. Then they rise to the top to form a layer above the water. You can even try to shake, stir, beat, or blend these substances. But no matter how hard you shake, stir, beat, or blend them, oil and water just won't mix! Do you know why? The answer has to do with the molecules that make up water and oil.

A molecule of water forms when one oxygen atom joins with two hydrogen atoms. To understand how they join together, it's important to remember what the inside of an atom looks like. At the very center is the nucleus, packed with protons and neutrons. Electrons whirl around outside the nucleus at different energy levels.

A hydrogen atom has only one electron in its outer energy level, but it needs two electrons to fill this level. An oxygen atom has six electrons in its outer energy level but needs eight. So what do these atoms do? They share electrons. Two hydrogen atoms join with one oxygen atom. As each hydrogen atom "plugs" its electron into the outer level of the oxygen atom, the oxygen gains the two electrons it needs to have eight in its outer shell. At the same time, the oxygen atom shares an electron with each hydrogen atom, giving each of them two electrons in their outer shell. Now everybody's happy! This friendship of one oxygen atom with two hydrogen atoms produces a water molecule. The hydrogen atoms look like Mickey Mouse ears sticking out on top of the oxygen atom, because the hydrogen atoms are smaller than the oxygen atom.

Because of the way the hydrogen atoms attach to the oxygen atom, the water molecule has a slightly positive charge on the "ear" end. The other end of the molecule— the "chin"—has a slightly negative charge. A molecule that has a positive charge on

> Did you receive the Holy Spirit by obeying the law? Or did you receive the Spirit by believing what you heard? Are you so foolish? You began with the Holy Spirit. Are you now trying to complete God's work in you by your own strength?
>
> GALATIANS 3:2–3

one end and a negative charge on the other is called a **polar** molecule. These charges cause water molecules to stick together—the positive end of one molecule is attracted to the negative end of another. These charges are also at work to help water mix with other kinds of molecules.

What does this have to do with oil and water? Molecules of water have charges, but molecules of oil don't—they're **nonpolar.** Because there are no overall charges in oil molecules, water molecules are attracted to each other and not the oil. The nonpolar oil molecules are also attracted to each other, but not to the polar water molecules. That's why oil and water don't mix. No matter how hard you shake, stir, beat, or blend oil and water, they always separate.

Oil and water don't mix. Did you know that there are other things in our lives that don't mix, either?

Maybe you've read about the **Israelites** in the Old Testament. They were a group of people whom God chose to follow Him, also known as Jews. The Israelites promised God they'd obey all the rules, or laws, He set. You may have heard of a few of these laws, called the Ten Commandments. It's impossible to follow *all* of God's rules without breaking them. Breaking one is called sin. If an Israelite sinned, he always had to make it right with God by offering a sacrifice.

Then Jesus was born. In the New Testament we find out that Jesus lived His life without ever sinning. Then He paid for all *our* sins by dying on a cross. Jesus measured up to the law for us because we couldn't do it ourselves. He took care of it for us by taking it out of the way. This is called **grace**. A way to remember what grace means is to think of this saying: "**G**od's **R**iches **A**t **C**hrist's **E**xpense." Jesus Christ did everything for us. Our job is simply to believe that He did. All we have to do is believe it's true.

Like oil and water, law and grace don't mix. When we try to please God by following the law, we depend on our own strength and our own good works. The problem is, our own works aren't good enough for God. What pleases God is for us to depend on what He has done—and will do—for us.

Sometimes we get confused, though. We come to God by

---

polar:
(POE-LuR)

nonpolar:
(NON-poe-LuR)

Israelite:
(IZ-Ree-uH-Lite)

grace: (RHymes with Place)

The PuRpose of the Law is to make us aware of our sin and our need for Jesus (see Romans 3:20).

There are some basic rules that explain which kinds of substances mix together:

* Two polar substances mix together. An example is water and sugar.

* Two *non*polar substances often mix together. An example is oil-based paint and paint thinner.

* A polar and nonpolar substance won't mix together.

* Soap removes oil from dishes because it has a polar and a nonpolar end. The polar end mixes with water, and the nonpolar end mixes with grease. That's why we add soap to water to clean our dishes!

TRy It!

See for yourself how oil and water don't mix. All you need is a jar with a lid, water, food coloring, and cooking oil. Pour water into the jar. Squeeze a few drops of your favorite food coloring into the water and blend. Now add oil to the water. Tightly replace the lid and gently shake the jar. What does the oil do? Shake the jar with more force. How does the combination of water and oil look now? How long does it take for the oil to rise to the top?

65

DIG DEEPER!

★ chemistry, solutions
★ water
★ molecules

believing in Jesus, and then we try to satisfy God by following His laws. Why should we try to live up to the law that condemns us? Jesus has set us free from the law!

Does this mean we can take advantage of God's grace and live any way we want, sinning if we feel like it? No! If we really understand how great Jesus' suffering was and how great His love is for us, we won't want to take advantage of His grace.

God wants us to come to Him by believing in Jesus. Then He wants us to keep on believing in Jesus to live a life that is pleasing to Him.

Thought to remember:

Believing in Jesus makes me right with God.

Additional verses:

John 6:28–29; Romans 3:20; 6:14; 2 Corinthians 8:9; Galatians 2:20–21; 5:13–14, 18; Philippians 3:9; Colossians 2:6

25 Canceled Out

f you've ever explored a dictionary, then you've noticed
that some words have a rainbow of meanings. The word **neutral** is that way. Black, white, and gray are neutral colors. A person who doesn't take sides in an argument is neutral. In the world of physics, certain particles that don't have electrical charges—neutrons—are neutral. In the world of chemistry, substances are neutral if they aren't acids or bases. What are acids and bases?

Let's start with acids. You'd recognize some of them by taste. They're the sour in foods such as lemons and limes. Coffee, tea, milk, vinegar, and soft drinks are also in this group. Extra-strong acids, such as battery acid and the powerful juices that digest food in your stomach, have a bite. They can burn your skin or eat holes through your clothing.

The word *acid* is like the word *neutral*—it can be defined in several ways by chemists. The simplest way is to talk about what happens when an acid is put in water. Acids produce positive hydrogen **ions** in water. Stronger acids produce more positive hydrogen ions in water.

Bases are sort of the opposite of acids. You'd recognize some by feel. Slippery and slimy, they're found in all sorts of soaps and cleaning products, even toothpaste. Also, bases are bitter tasting. Baking soda is a weak base that makes cakes and cookies fluffy.

> "Come. Let us talk some more about this matter," says the Lord. "Even though your sins are bright red, they will be as white as snow. Even though they are deep red, they will be white like wool."
>
> ISAIAH 1:18

What makes a base? In water, a base produces a negatively charged ion formed of one oxygen and one hydrogen atom that join together. Stronger bases produce more of these negative ions in water.

Something special happens when acids are added to bases. They cancel each other out, or **neutralize** each other. What do you get when one positive hydrogen ion joins with a negative ion of oxygen and hydrogen? A molecule made up of one oxygen and two hydrogen atoms. H_2O. Neutral water!

In the world of chemistry, when acids and bases join, they neutralize each other, or completely "cancel" each other out. Something similar takes place in the spiritual

neutral:
(NEW-trul)

ion: (EYE-on)
an atom or molecule that has gained or lost one or more electrons, giving it a negative or positive charge

neutralize:
(NEW-truh-lies)

Any other chemicals in the solution besides the oxygen and hydrogen also combine; they form what's called a salt.

Chemists have a special way to measure how strong an acid or base is. They use a **pH** (pea-aitch) scale. This scale is numbered from one to fourteen. The middle of the scale, seven, is neutral. Numbers larger than seven are basic; fourteen is the strongest. Numbers smaller than seven are acidic; one is the strongest. Here are some pH numbers of common items:

stomach acid 2	pure water 7
soft drinks 3	blood 7½
lemon juice 3½	seawater 8
grapes 4	soap 9½
bread 5½	ammonia 11
milk 6	oven cleaner 14

Make It!

It's not safe to identify acids and bases by tasting or feeling them! That's why chemists use **indicators** (IN-dih-kay-ters) to tell them apart. With the help of an adult, make your own acid/base indicator. All you need is a red cabbage and several small jars or glasses. Cut the cabbage into small pieces, place the pieces in a pot, cover them with water, and bring it all to a boil. Then let the solution cool.

Pour a small amount of cabbage water into each container.

Add a small amount of lemon juice to one jar and a teaspoonful of baking soda to another. What color does the cabbage water turn?

Lemon juice is an acid; it turns the water pink. Baking soda is a base; it turns the water green. Experiment with other substances such as vinegar, milk, ammonia, glass cleaner, and orange juice.

DIG DEEPER!

* acids and bases
* chemistry

world, too.

Every human in this world is born with a problem. That problem is sin. We're all born wanting to run our lives our own way instead of God's way. Sin keeps us from being close to God. He is pure and holy and won't allow sin in His presence. Because God wants us to be close to Him, though, He gave us an answer to our problem. He sent His Son, Jesus, to "neutralize" our sins completely. Jesus did that when He paid for our sins on the cross. Every single sin has been completely canceled out, just as an acid cancels out a base. As we turn from running our lives our own way and believe that Jesus neutralized our sins, all our sins are forgiven. God won't hold them against us; our guilt is completely, one hundred percent gone. When our sins are neutralized, we have new lives.

We've been forgiven so much—more than we can ever understand. Since God's forgiveness is so amazingly generous, He wants us to forgive others who hurt us. He says that love covers a great number of sins (see 1 Peter 4:8).

If you have a hard time forgiving someone, remember that Jesus neutralized *all* your sins.

Thought to remember:
Jesus neutralized all my sins.

Additional verses:
Isaiah 53:4–6; Matthew 18:21–22; Acts 3:19; Romans 8:1; Colossians 2:13–14; 3:13; Hebrews 8:12; Revelation 1:5b

26 Inside, Outside, All Around

Here's a riddle:

You can't see, taste, or smell me.
You can't live without me.
I'm inside, outside, and all around you.
What am I?

Air.

Most people aren't even aware of air, that stuff we breathe twelve to fifteen times a minute, twenty-four hours a day. Yet it's a critical part of our lives. The blanket of air surrounding the earth protects us from harmful rays of the sun and space objects that would bombard us. It traps heat from the sun to keep us warm. Air is the invisible substance that helps turn the sky blue and allows clouds to form. It's also the substance sound waves travel through . . . and jets, birds, and lots of bugs, too.

Just as our bodies are made up of certain chemical elements, so is air. The gases in air are made mostly of nitrogen molecules. A whopping seventy-eight out of a hundred parts—or seventy-eight percent—are nitrogen. Another gas, oxygen, comes in second at twenty-one percent. Several other gases are also present, but barely there, in air.

> On that day you will realize that I am in my Father. You will know that you are in me, and I am in you.
>
> JOHN 14:20

On a trip up through the atmosphere, we'll discover that the earth wears air in layers. The **troposphere**, the first layer, lies closest to the earth's surface. It's rich with nitrogen and oxygen, the gases needed to support life. Most of the earth's weather action takes place here in the troposphere.

But as we rise above the troposphere and into the **stratosphere**, we notice that the air thins out. Very few clouds hang out here. We also notice that the stratosphere is home to the atmosphere's **ozone**—which absorbs most of the sun's harmful rays.

Climbing higher still, we reach the **mesosphere**. Do you notice that as we rise in altitude, the temperature decreases? Not much sunlight is absorbed in this windy layer where temperatures plunge well below minus one hundred degrees Fahrenheit.

Brr. To escape the chill, we only have to drift higher into the **thermosphere**, where the air is rare. This layer is so exposed to the extremes of the sun's heat that tem-

The gases that form air are constantly being removed from the atmosphere. So why don't we run out of air? As much as they're removed, they're replaced. Wherever air is found, this invisible substance is basically made up of the same amounts of nitrogen and oxygen. Amazing!

Discover It!

Try this experiment to show the presence of air all around us. You will need a small jar and a sink full of water.

Fill the sink with enough water to cover the jar. Turn the jar upside down. Keeping the mouth level, lower the jar into the water. Now tilt the jar slightly. You will hear a *BLURP* as a large bubble rises to the surface of the water. Tilt the jar several more times until only a small bubble remains at the top of the upside-down jar. When the jar is lowered into the water, air is trapped inside. It escapes when the jar is tilted.

DIG DEEPER!

* air
* atmosphere
* sky

---

peratures may rocket to well over one thousand degrees! The bottom part of the thermosphere is the **ionosphere**. Sunrays strike atoms at this level to produce electrically charged particles called ions. Ions are important to radio communication because they bounce radio waves back to earth.

Beyond the thermosphere is the outermost layer, a place where there's barely any air. Welcome to the **exosphere**, where atoms and molecules that form air can escape the pull of the earth's gravity and float off into space.

> Here's another riddle:
> You can't see, smell, or taste me.
> You can't live without me.
> I'm inside, outside, and all around you.
> Who am I?
> *Jesus.*

Many people aren't aware of Jesus, the giver of those breaths we take twelve to fifteen times a minute, twenty-four hours a day. As much as we need air, we need Jesus more. Not only does His Spirit breathe physical and spiritual life into us, He also gives us a reason to live.

Although a lot of people aren't aware of Jesus, He's very close to those who come to God, the Father, through Him. He's not a faraway God. In fact, Jesus is so close you could say He's as close as air. Like air, He surrounds you . . . He's inside you . . . you're in Him and He's in you. You can't be any closer than that!

No matter what problems pop up in your life—trouble with teachers, fights with friends, fumbling families—always remember that Jesus and you are as close as can be. The two of you are one, so you're in this together. Nothing happens to you that doesn't happen to Him. No matter what situation you're in, remember that Jesus' love blankets you. His love will bring you peace.

Thought to remember:

Jesus and I are as close as can be. I am in Him, and He is in me.

Additional verses:

Acts 17:28a; Romans 8:38–39; 1 Corinthians 6:17; Galatians 2:20; Colossians 1:27; 1 John 4:13–16

---

ionosphere: (eye-ON-uh-sfear)

exosphere: (EK-so-sfear) The exosphere extends three hundred to one thousand miles above the earth.

What keeps air from floating away into space? The same force that holds us here—gravity.

Are gases the only substances in our atmosphere? No! The earth's atmosphere also carries water vapor, salt from sea spray, microscopic organisms, plus "dust" particles from soil, fires, and volcanoes.

27 A Whisper of Wind

Suppose you were given the important job of sending winds out over the earth. A soft sigh of wind could soothe those suffering from the heat of the day. A lion's roar of wind could rip off roofs, push over trees, steal soil from farmers, or cause giant waves to bash boats. With wind you could gather clouds to bring rains to a thirsty world. Or blow them away to dry the world off again.

Wind is a powerful force! How would you create it?

By getting air to move.

Begin by bathing the earth with heat from the sun. As the earth's surface heats up, some of this heat passes to the air just above it. Heated air molecules jostle about with more energy, spreading apart from each other. This results in lighter air that rises from the earth. While warm air rises, colder, heavier air—from areas that aren't as warm—rushes in to take its place. Now you've got moving air—or wind!

Along with temperature, air pressure also has a part in creating wind. Warm, light, rising air pushes against the earth with less pressure than cold, heavy, sinking air. So we can say that warm air is linked to low pressure. Cold air is linked to high pressure. High-pressure air always sweeps in toward areas of low pressure to create wind.

Since the sun warms certain parts of the earth more than others, there's a pattern to the winds that tickle our planet. Take the equator. This part of the world receives more warmth than any other part of the world. Since warm air is lighter, the earth wears a belt of low pressure around its middle. This warmed air rises and moves north and south. Partway there, some of the air cools and sinks, looping back toward the equator—to take the place of rising warm air again. These dependable winds are called trade winds.

Wind patterns also exist at local levels where land heats and cools during the day. In the morning, mountainsides heat up more quickly than valleys below. Since warm, low-pressure air rises, cooler air from the valleys creeps up slopes and creates a **breeze**. The opposite also happens at night. Cool air coasts down mountainsides and into valleys.

Here's a jingle to help you remember how temperature affects the movement of air: "Warm air is light, and rises into space. Cold air sinks down, rushing in to take its place."

> The wind blows where it wants to. You hear the sound it makes. But you can't tell where it comes from or where it is going. It is the same with everyone who is born through the Spirit.
>
> JOHN 3:8

breeze: a gentle wind

Here is more wind trivia:

* You can tell where a breeze comes from by its name. Valley breezes flow up a mountainside from the valley. Mountain breezes start in the mountain and flow down. Sea breezes begin out at sea. And where do land breezes begin?

* The **doldrums** (DOLE-drums) are ocean areas near the equator with light, unpredictable winds and sudden storms. In the past, sailors avoided these areas; they couldn't sail when the winds died down.

* Other areas with undependable winds are called horse **latitudes** (LAT-uh-tudes). Where did this name come from? Horses were thrown overboard when sailing ships stalled because of lack of wind.

DiSCOVeR It!

To discover how warm air rises, you will need an empty glass soda bottle, a balloon, and a pan with hot water. (Ask an adult to help with this activity!)

Stretch the balloon over the neck of the bottle. Place the bottle in the pan of hot water and place it on a stove burner. Turn the burner on low. What happens to the balloon as warm air rises into it?

DIG DEEPER!

* wind
* weather
* air

Temperature and pressure differences between land and water also create breezes. During the day, land heats to a higher temperature than the nearby ocean. By late afternoon a sea breeze whispers from water to land. And overnight when the land cools more than the water? Land breezes drift from cooler land to warmer water.

No matter which direction a wind blows because of temperature and pressure differences, two things are true: We can't see wind, and we can't control it. But we can see leaves flutter in breezes. We can feel the wind as it puffs at our faces. We can hear light winds whisper in the trees.

In surprising ways, the wind reminds us of the Holy Spirit. We can't see Him, because He is a spirit. We can't control Him, either, because He is God. Yet we see His influence in our lives and the lives of those around us. He's like a powerful wind as He shows us our sin and stirs our hearts to come to God. He's like a gentle breeze as He whispers which way we should go. His words encourage, comfort, and teach us along the way. We sense His presence with us as He brings joy, peace, and courage into our lives, and as He whisks away fears. No wonder Jesus used the wind to teach a man named **Nicodemus** about the Holy Spirit (see John 3:8).

Nicodemus: (Nih-KO-DEE-mus)

Unlike the wind, though, the Spirit of God is personal. He comes to live inside us when we believe in Jesus. In spite of the fact that we can't see Him, we can get to know Him. We can grow close to Him as we pay attention to His movement in our lives. And when we have bad attitudes or we're unloving toward others, we can even grieve the Holy Spirit. He wouldn't feel sad if He didn't care about us, would He?

Just like the wind, you can't see the Holy Spirit. But if you watch, you'll see His influence in your life.

Thought to remember:

The Holy Spirit is like the wind. We can't see Him, but we can see His work in our lives.

Additional verses:

John 14:26 (NIV); Acts 9:31; 13:52; Romans 5:5; 14:17; 1 Corinthians 6:19; Ephesians 4:30

28 A Cat, a King, an Angel's Wing

You'll find them floating through the air—
Lions, tigers, wolves, and bears.
A piece of pie, a ball, a boat,
An elephant, a scruffy goat.
A swan, a fox, a fluffy mouse,
A hog that turns into a house.
A chimpanzee, a lion's face,
A train that vanishes without a trace.
A cat, a king, an angel's wing.
Clouds can be just anything!

evaporate:
(ee-VAP-or-ate)
to turn from a
liquid into a gas

condense:
(kun-DENTS)

Air also cools
when a body of
warm air meets a
body of cold air,
when wind carries
warm air over
cold water or
land, and when
air is forced up
the side of a
mountain.

stratus: (STRAY-
tus or STRAT-us)
comes from the
word "strato,"
which means
"sheetlike" or
"layered"

Where does the endless parade of clouds come from? A cloud begins to form when water **evaporates** from oceans, lakes, rivers, and plants. Once water turns into an invisible gas called water vapor, it floats through the air. If the air is warm, it carries the water vapor higher and higher into the sky, expanding as it goes. Then, at a certain point, the air begins to cool. Since cool air can't hold as much moisture as warm air, the water vapor **condenses**, or turns back to liquid in the form of water droplets.

Like beads of water that condense on the outside of your iced tea glass on a hot day, water vapor also has to have something to condense onto. What can water vapor attach to thousands of feet above the earth? Dust . . . salt . . . tiny particles from smoke . . . and even ice. Water droplets that condense on these itty-bitty particles form the clouds we see as crocodiles and cockatoos, ice cream cones and kangaroos.

> May the God of hope fill you with all joy and peace as you trust in Him, so that you may overflow with hope by the power of the Holy Spirit.
>
> ROMANS 15:13 (NIV)

As you scan the sky, you'll notice there are different types of clouds. Basically there are three kinds, as well as combinations of all three.

Clouds that form layers are called **stratus** clouds. They form low, smooth sheets that blanket the sky and block out the sun. If any moisture falls from stratus clouds, it's usually a fine rain called drizzle.

Clouds that form ships and shoes and big baboons in the midregions of the sky are

Clouds are made of water droplets, but how do raindrops form? Large droplets bump into smaller ones, joining to form a raindrop that eventually becomes too heavy and falls from the cloud.

Raindrops also grow when water droplets freeze directly onto ice crystals. As enlarged ice crystals fall from the cloud, they melt and turn to rain.

What is fog? A cloud that forms near the surface of the earth. Fog forms when water vapor condenses close to the ground.

What is smog? Fog mixed with smoke and chemical particles.

Explore It!

On a hot day, fill a glass with ice water. Wait a few minutes. Does the outside of the glass look as if it's sweating?

The beads of water that form on the outside of your glass come from moisture in the air. As warm air next to the icy glass cools, it can't hold as much moisture. The water vapor then condenses on your glass.

DIG DEEPER!

* clouds
* weather

---

cumulus clouds. These thick piles of clouds have puffy, billowy tops. And when they mushroom into mountainous dark clouds with flat tops, watch out! **Cumulonimbus** clouds often come loaded with rain, thunder, and lightning.

If you look high in the sky where the air is always cold, you'll spot **cirrus** clouds. These thin and wispy clouds are made completely of ice crystals. Sometimes they look like flowing horse tails. When you see cirrus clouds, you may want to take them "cirrious," because they often signal a change in weather.

From day to day, clouds grow in the skies around us. From day to day, clouds also grow in the skies of our lives. Perhaps some of these clouds hover over you right now. Struggles with studies . . . getting along with friends, family members, or teammates . . . a sickness or health problem that—like a cloud—threatens to hang around forever . . . the loss of a parent's job . . . your parents' divorce . . . the death of someone close.

Just as clouds sometimes last for days or weeks, the clouds of our lives can, too. And just as these dark clouds can block the warmth and light of the sun, the clouds of our lives can also block the warmth and light of Jesus, the Son. We can begin to wonder whether we'll see Jesus' light again. We can even begin to wonder if He's still in our lives!

If you're wondering whether the Son of God is really still in your life, be encouraged. He is! Just as you know that the sun is always there—even if clouds block its warmth—you can be sure that Jesus is still in your life, too. There are times when you simply have to have **faith** that Jesus is with you, even though you don't feel Him or see Him work in your life.

Overcast days may not be pleasant to go through. But believing Jesus is with us, even when we can't see or feel Him, can make any gray day bright.

Thought to remember:
God is with me, even when I can't feel Him or see His work in my life.

Additional verses:
Joshua 1:9; Psalm 16:11; 56:3; Hebrews 11

CUMULUS: (KYU-myuh-lus) comes from the word "cumulo," which means "piled" or "heaped"

CUMULONIMBUS: (KYU-myuh-low-NIM-bus)

CIRRUS: (SEAR-us) comes from the word "cirro," which means "curly"

faith: to believe or trust; being sure something is true, even though we can't see it

㉙ THUNDER POWER

Have you ever heard "bug thunder"? Chances are you have, if you've ever shuffled your feet along carpet and then touched a metal doorknob—or given your mom a kiss. Ouch! That surprising little spark and the tiny *snap* that accompanied it were actually lightning and thunder—bug-sized lightning and thunder.

Believe it or not, the cause of the tiny shock in your home is the same as for lightning on a stormy afternoon. Both are caused by a buildup of electrical charges. A lot of it has to do with the fact that positive and negative charges attract each other. When you shuffle your feet along carpet, you lose electrons and become positively charged. Touching a negatively charged doorknob causes a release of electrical energy, creating a tiny spark of lightning and the *snap* of bug thunder!

The same thing happens in clouds. On summer days, hot moist air rises from the earth to form towering cumulonimbus clouds. Scientists aren't sure why, but positive charges often form at the top of clouds, while negative charges gather at the bottom. If the buildup of charges becomes great enough, a giant spark—or lightning—flashes inside a cloud or between two clouds.

Most lightning takes place among the clouds, but the strikes we're most aware of are the jagged bolts that flash between clouds and earth. In order for that to happen, the earth must become charged. How?

The negative charges in the bottom of clouds influence the electrical charges on earth. They encourage the earth's positive charges to draw closer to the surface of the earth. At the same time, the earth's negative charges are repelled. They migrate away from the surface. If enough charges in the clouds and on the earth's surface build up, a streak of light splits the sky and, *BOOM*, thunder follows.

It all happens so fast that we don't realize there are actually several stages to the flashes we see. First, negative electrons travel toward the earth in a series of steps. This is called a stepped leader. When the fork-shaped stepped leader gets close enough to the ground, positive charges from the earth jump up to meet it and form a channel.

Some scientists think raindrops and ice particles pick up charges as they smash into each other. Heavier, negatively charged particles then sink to the bottom of the cloud.

> WHEN I HEAR THE THUNDER, MY HEART POUNDS. IT beats faster inside me. GOD'S voice THUNDERS IN WONDERFUL WAYS. WE'LL NEVER UNDERSTAND THE great things HE DOES.
>
> JOB 37:1, 5

Be "lightning alert."
During a lightning storm

* move away from single
  tall trees in open areas.
  If there's no building or
  car for shelter, take
  cover under low bushes
  or in a *group* of trees of
  the same height.

* if you're caught out in
  the open, crouch down
  or sit, but don't let your
  hands touch the
  ground.

* avoid the tops of hills or
  mountains.

* stay away from water
  and metal objects.

CHECK IT OUT!

You can use
thunder to fig-
ure out how
far away light-
ning is. When
you see a flash, count the
number of seconds until
you hear thunder. Divide
that number by five to tell
you how many miles away
the lightning was. Suppose
you counted ten seconds
between lightning and
thunder. Ten divided by five
is two, so the lightning
strike was two miles away.

DIG DEEPER!

* lightning
* thunder
* weather
  and climate

Charges then instantly rush along the channel in a return stroke, lighting the sky. Sometimes a series of return strokes takes place along the same path, which is why lightning sometimes seems to flicker.

These storm-cloud fireworks can heat the air to a scorching 50,000 degrees Fahrenheit! The heated air explodes into the surrounding cooler air, creating the *BOOM* we call thunder. If close enough, its sharp crack can make us hit the deck. But whether it's a deafening blast or a distant rumble, thunder warns us to watch out. It isn't something we can ignore or take lightly!

God sometimes uses lightning and thunder when He talks about himself. His voice thunders (see Job 37:4–5). Both thunder and lightning are present at His throne (see Revelation 4:5) and at some of His works here on earth (see Psalm 77:18). Why do you think God uses thunder and lightning to describe himself?

Could it be that He doesn't want us to take Him lightly, either? By describing himself with thunder and lightning, we get a sense of His greatness and awesome power. Thunder and lightning give us the idea that God is **holy** and that we'd better take Him seriously. Just as thunder and lightning can amaze and make us tremble, God also amazes us. He makes us tremble.

Trembling before God isn't a bad thing! It means that we have some understanding of how great He is—and that we are merely people. It causes us to honor and worship Him.

God wants us to come near to Him. But in coming close to God, we don't want to forget that He is God and that we need to respect Him.

Who is God to you? The next time rolling thunder shakes your skies, remember His greatness and worship Him!

Thought to remember:
God is mighty and powerful!

Additional verses:
Job 37:1–5; 40:9; Psalm 29:3–4; Joel 3:16;
Revelation 4:5

Lightning releases about 100 million volts of electricity. We use a measly 120 volts for most of our electrical appliances—and that's enough to kill us!

Light travels at about 186,000 miles per second. Sound travels at a snail's pace of only 1,116 feet per second, taking about 5 seconds to travel one mile. That's why thunder reaches us after we see the lightning.

Holy: perfectly pure and blameless

Every year monsters are born in ocean waters near the equator. They crawl across open seas toward land, growing so large and powerful that humans watch their approach with fear. Nothing can stop them—planes, radar, and satellites can only track their progress and warn people when to flee. Hitting land, these beasts uproot trees and tear apart houses, swallowing whole cities that lie in their paths.

What are these terrifying monsters? Hurricanes, the most violent storms on earth. Let's see how they're born.

For a hurricane to come to life, ocean waters must be warm—at least eighty degrees Fahrenheit. The air must be hot and **humid**; high-level winds must be gentle. Birth begins when warm water evaporates and rises. Once the air cools, clouds form. As water vapor turns into water droplets that form clouds, heat is given off. This causes the air to become lighter and rise even higher. More clouds form. Air rushes in from below to take the place of the rising air, creating winds that swirl around a center. Meanwhile, a high-pressure area above the storm funnels air out of the top of the hurricane. More moist air is drawn into the building storm; winds blow harder. When they reach seventy-four miles per hour, the storm is considered a hurricane.

If you flew a plane toward the center of the storm, first you'd encounter miles of thick cloud arms called rainbands. These arms spiral around the middle of the hurricane, like a giant pinwheel, dropping sheets of rain. Next you'd bump into the eye wall, near the center of the storm. The plane seems more like a bucking bronco now, because the eye wall is a tower of thick clouds and violent winds. But if you keep going, you're in for a surprise. Breaking through the eye wall, you experience sunny skies; the plane coasts through miles of gentle winds. Is the storm over? No, this is the very center, the eye of the storm.

Winds would try to move into the low-pressure area at the eye, but the same force

---

Hurricanes are also known as typhoons, cyclones, and willy-willies in other parts of the world.

Humid: (HYU-mid) containing moisture

To discover more about how clouds form, turn to "A Cat, a King, an Angel's Wing," on page 73.

What causes winds to spin? The spinning of the earth! In the Northern Hemisphere they turn counterclockwise. In the Southern Hemisphere they turn clockwise. This is called the Coriolis (KORE-ee-OH-lus) effect.

Then they cried out to the LORD in their trouble, and He brought them out of their distress. He stilled the storm to a whisper; the waves of the sea were hushed.

PSALM 107:28–29

Hurricane winds can cause a lot of damage, but water often does more. The low pressure of the storm's eye pulls ocean water up into a large bulge called a surge. When the surge hits the coastline, the bulge drops, flooding homes and drowning people who haven't fled. Add gushing rains and huge waves whipped up by powerful winds, and you can see why hurricane waters can pack a wallop!

People keep track of hurricanes by giving them names. Alphabetical lists of men and women are kept on hand as storms form. Names of deadly storms are dropped from the lists.

Think About It!

Do you have a hurricane raging through your life? Get your Bible and find a quiet, cozy spot where you won't be disturbed. Open your Bible and slowly read the verses listed under **Additional verses** on this page. If you want, close your eyes and pour out your heart to God. Tell Him about all of the troubles that make you feel unsettled and churned up inside. Now think about the God who lives inside you and is able to "still the storm to a whisper" and hush the waves of the sea. He is greater than all your problems. Give them to Jesus. Trade your stormy feelings for His quiet peace.

Dig Deeper!

* hurricane
* tropical cyclone
* typhoon
* weather
* natural disasters

that pushes us away from the center of a twirling merry-go-round "pushes" winds out from the center. Plus, some of the rising air sinks back down into this center column. As this sinking air presses together, it heats up. Since warm air can carry more moisture, clouds don't form and the eye becomes nearly cloud-free. Of course, if you keep flying you'll hit the surrounding eye wall again, then more rainbands.

You can see why these storms that can grow into five-hundred-mile-wide monsters leave destruction wherever they travel. Fortunately, once hurricanes cross land or travel over cooler waters, they begin to die. But even a hurricane's short seven- to fourteen-day life-span is much too long if it crashes through your neighborhood!

Do you ever feel as if a hurricane's ripping through your life? All kinds of problems and changes can make it seem that way. Perhaps . . .

* your parents are getting divorced. Traveling between two homes makes you feel like a yo-yo.

* a sickness threatens the life of a family member.

* a brother or sister is having serious problems.

* your mother or dad is always mad at you; it seems as if you can't do anything right.

Even changes such as moving to a new school or losing a good friend can destroy the peace in your life.

While we live in this world, every one of us experiences storms that overwhelm us. Sometimes we wish God would make them disappear, or that we could fly away like a bird. But Jesus doesn't promise to take them all away. He has overcome them. If you're in one of life's hurricanes, remember that just as every hurricane has an eye, every storm in your life has an eye, too. Jesus is the eye of your storms. He's the place of calm and sunshine even while the wild winds of change and trouble swirl around you.

If you're in a hurricane, look to Jesus. Go deep inside, past the hurts and disappointments, to His love. He'll be your peace in the midst of any storm.

Thought to remember:

Jesus gives me peace in the midst of any storm.

Additional verses:

Exodus 33:14; Psalm 32:7; 55:4–6, 16; Isaiah 25:4; Luke 8:22–25; John 14:27

31 Solid as a Rock

Picture a dog. Do you see a white, black, or tan dog? Is it spotted, striped, or plain? Are its ears short and pointy or long and floppy? Was the dog you pictured a **Chihuahua**, a Labrador retriever, or a mutt?

The word *dog* brings to mind all kinds of colors, shapes, and sizes!

Now picture a rock. If you've never paid a lot of attention to rocks, you might imagine something hard, gray, and small enough to hold in your hand. To many people a rock is a rock.

But it's not! Just as there are many kinds of dogs, there are also many kinds of rocks. The differences come from what they're made of and how they're formed.

The building blocks of rocks are minerals, solid nonliving materials found naturally in the earth. Minerals can be formed of a single element such as carbon. Or they can be formed of two or more elements, such as oxygen and **silicon**.

Different rocks are made of groupings of different minerals. **Granite** is basically made of the minerals **quartz**, feldspar, and **mica**. Sandstone is made of the minerals quartz and calcite. Slate is made of quartz, mica, and **chlorite**. Granite, sandstone, and slate all have quartz in them. Granite and slate also have mica. Adding other minerals gives each rock its individuality. And how they're made also makes each one distinct.

Granite is an **igneous** rock. It's formed of melted rock—or **magma**—deep inside the earth, where it cools slowly. This type of igneous rock develops out of sight, but another kind takes shape right before our eyes. When magma reaches the surface of the earth, we call it lava. Volcanoes may spew fiery lava high into the sky. Or lava may seep from cracks in the earth. The speed with which lava cools also gives us different kinds of rock. **Pumice** is an igneous rock that forms from lava. It's super lightweight because gas bubbles get trapped in the lava as it cools.

Sandstone belongs to a second family of rocks, the **sedimentary** family. Rocks on the surface of the earth are constantly exposed to wind, water, and ice. Slowly these forces break rocks down to smaller bits, or *sediments*, such as pebbles, sand, and clay. The same forces that wear down rocks also carry the sediments away. Eventually the particles settle and form layers. The upper layers then press down on the sediments in the lower layers and turn them to stone. Water may also carry minerals down through the

Chihuahua: (chih-WAH-wuh)

Silicon: (SILL-ih-kun)

Granite: (GRAN-it)

quartz: (KWARTS)

mica: (MY-kuh)

chlorite: (KLORE-ite)

igneous: (IG-nee-us) comes from a word that means "fire"

magma: (MAG-muh)

Pumice: (PUH-miss)

Sedimentary: (Said-ih-MEN-tuh-Ree) comes from a word that means "to sink down"

> **There is no Rock like our God.**
>
> 1 SAMUEL 2:2b

79

Rocks can change from one family to another. This is called the rock cycle. Here are some examples: Igneous rocks can change into sedimentary, to metamorphic, then to igneous rocks again. Sedimentary rocks can change into other sedimentary rocks. Metamorphic rocks can change into sedimentary rocks. Igneous rocks can change into metamorphic rocks.

FIND It!

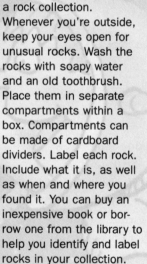

Here are some suggestions to help you start a rock collection. Whenever you're outside, keep your eyes open for unusual rocks. Wash the rocks with soapy water and an old toothbrush. Place them in separate compartments within a box. Compartments can be made of cardboard dividers. Label each rock. Include what it is, as well as when and where you found it. You can buy an inexpensive book or borrow one from the library to help you identify and label rocks in your collection.

DIG DEEPER!

* rocks
* minerals
* igneous
* sedimentary
* metamorphic

sediments to cement them together. Some sedimentary rocks form from the remains of plants and animals. Coal is made from buried plants. Chalk is made from shells of tiny ocean animals.

Slate is an example of a third family, **metamorphic** rocks. Metamorphic rocks form when changes take place in rocks that already exist. Add heat to a sedimentary rock called shale, and you get a new rock—slate. The heat comes from magma and hot gases that force their way up through the shale. Marble, a common metamorphic rock used in sculptures, is formed when magma comes in contact with another rock, limestone. But heat isn't the only force that transforms rocks. The weight of the earth and movement of its crust produce extreme pressures that also create metamorphic rocks.

metamorphic: (meh-tuh-MORE-fik) comes from a word that means "to change form"

Many kinds of rocks are born of magma, sediments, heat, and pressure. But when we think of rocks, most of us probably don't think about how they came about. We tend to think of qualities that many rocks share. Most rocks are firm and solid, not easily broken. Large towers and mountains of rock are not easily moved; they give a sense of strength and power. They shield us and give us safety, support, and security.

In the Bible God is often called the Rock. In fact, it is one of His names. Why do you think Rock is one of His names? Could it be because . . .

* He's much stronger and more powerful than we are?

* He can't be broken or overcome by man?

* He is unmovable, and this gives us a sense of safety, support, and security?

All of us need someone we can depend on. Why not turn to God? He is the Rock our Savior (see 2 Samuel 22:47). He is the Rock, our fortress and deliverer, a safe place to hide (see Psalm 18:2). He is the Rock who keeps our lives from sinking and gives us a firm place to stand (see Psalm 40:2). There is no Rock like our God (see 1 Samuel 2:2)!

Thought to remember:

God is my Rock!

Additional verses:

2 Samuel 22:32–34; Psalm 18:1–2; 62:5-8; 89:26; Isaiah 26:4 (NIV)

What picture do you think pops into most people's

minds when they hear the word *treasure*? For many the picture might be a pirate's chest overflowing with gold coins, strings of pearls, and rings set with rubies, emeralds, and diamonds. Or it might be a sunken ship with jewels scattered on the ocean floor.

Wherever you go in the world, most people probably recognize gold, silver, and gems as treasures. There are reasons that gold and silver, and emeralds, rubies, and diamonds are so valuable. Can you think of a few?

More than anything they're beautiful. They sparkle and shine, and we like to decorate ourselves with them. Most of them are also pretty hard and tough; they last a long time even when worn daily. A third reason certain metals and jewels are so precious is because they're rare. Finding them is hard, sometimes dangerous work.

Most of these special metals and gemstones are minerals. Minerals are solid nonliving materials that make up the earth's crust. They can be formed of one element such as carbon, the material diamonds are made of. Or minerals can be formed of two or more elements, such as aluminum and oxygen, the materials rubies and **sapphires** are made of. Here are a few tests used to identify gems and the minerals they're made of:

> "You will seek me and find me when you seek me with all your heart. I will be found by you," declares the Lord.
>
> JEREMIAH
> 29:13–14a

sapphire:
(SAF-ire)

unique: (you-neek)
one of a kind

cleavage:
(CLEE-vij)

The Mohs (MOZE) hardness scale compares minerals on a scale of one to ten. One is the softest. Ten is the hardest.

★ Minerals are made of crystals, each with a special shape. The crystal's structure comes from the **unique** 3-D way its atoms join together. The flat surfaces of crystals are what make some gems so beautiful.

★ **Cleavage**—the way a mineral is likely to break. Some minerals break evenly in more than one direction and produce flat, smooth surfaces. Diamonds break in four directions. The way a mineral breaks depends on its crystal structure.

★ Hardness—how easily a mineral scratches. The hardness of a mineral depends on how its atoms are arranged and bonded together. Diamonds are the hardest. Rubies and sapphires come in second.

★ Index of refraction—how light bends as it enters the gem. Diamonds are so glittery, or brilliant, because they bend light a lot. The way gemstones are cut also

Most gemstones are minerals, formed of nonliving materials. But pearls, **coral** (CORE-ul), amber, and jet come from plants and animals. Oysters create pearls when they coat sand and other small objects inside them with a pearly substance. Coral comes from the skeletons of small sea animals. Amber is tree sap, or **resin** (REH-zin) that has fossilized. Jet forms from rotted and compressed wood. It's similar to coal, but it can be carved and polished.

Check It Out!

Time for a trip to a jewelry store or the jewelry section of a department store. Take this list of gems with you. See how many you can find. Compare the colors of the same gems at different stores. Some gems may have more than one color.

* diamond
* jade
* sapphire
* pearl
* topaz
* ruby
* emerald
* aquamarine
* amethyst
* opal
* turquoise
* garnet

DIG DEEPER!

* gems and gemstones
* minerals
* crystals
* precious stones

affects how much they sparkle.

* **Dispersion**—how much a gem separates light into the colors of the rainbow, making them flash with color, or "fire."

Some people search the earth's surface for precious minerals brought up from the deep by volcanoes or water. But some are also willing to go underwater and underground on treasure hunts that could bring them wealth. Miners often sift through tons of rock to find one small stone. Many have even risked their lives in the quest for earth's hidden treasures.

It's easy to see why people search for earth's treasures. But there's another kind of treasure we can seek while we live here on earth. This treasure is worth more than the biggest and most sparkling of rubies, diamonds, or emeralds. This treasure is worth much more than all the world's gold, silver, and jewels put together. It doesn't break, scratch, discolor, or wear out. Far more beautiful and stunning than the finest of gems, nothing can compare with it. What is this treasure?

This treasure is God.

The seriousness of a person searching for precious metals and gemstones is a good example of a heart searching for God. In fact, God encourages us to search for Him even harder than we would search for earthly treasures. We search for Him with our whole hearts, as if our lives depend on it, as if nothing else in this world is important.

A person searching for earthly treasures isn't always rewarded with much more than sweat and weariness. But God promises to satisfy us when we search for Him. The delight of knowing God as He reveals himself to us through Jesus is greater than any joy out of earth's treasure chest. As we continue to seek God and get to know Him more deeply, He's much more satisfying than any treasure on earth!

Thought to remember:
God is our true treasure.

Additional verses:
Psalm 27:4, 8; 63:1–5; 105:3–4 (NIV); Proverbs 2:3–6; 9:10; Matthew 6:19–21; 7:7–8; Colossians 2:2–3

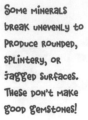

Some minerals break unevenly to produce rounded, splintery, or jagged surfaces. These don't make good gemstones!

DISPERSION: (dih-SPUR-zhun)

33 Dazzling Diamonds

The story begins in 1866.

A sparkly stone in a riverbank caught the attention of a fifteen-year-old South African boy, **Erasmus** Jacobs. Bringing the stone home, he and other kids played with it. One day, Erasmus's mother decided to give this unusual stone to a visitor who was curious about it. The white rock would have probably been forgotten if it hadn't ended up in the hands of a doctor who realized that this was much more than a pretty pebble. This glittering crystal was a large diamond.

The story of Erasmus's sparkly stone is important because it was the first of many diamonds discovered in the area. But it's even more important because South African diamonds eventually helped **geologists** understand the secrets of how these special stones form.

Erasmus:
(ih-RAZ-mus)

geologist:
(jee-ALL-uh-jist)
a scientist who
studies the earth

kimberlite:
(KIM-burr-lite)

The clues came from a type of rock, **kimberlite**, named after the South African town Kimberly, where it was first discovered. Diamonds are often found in and around kimberlite. Geologists believe that diamonds first form deep inside the earth. Here—up to 150 miles below the surface, where pressure and temperatures are great—conditions are just right to turn carbon into diamond crystals. At these super-high pressures and temperatures, each carbon atom bonds to four others in a tight arrangement that turns them into the hardest natural substance known to man.

How do these extra-hard crystals rise from such depths to the surface, where diamond diggers can

My brothers and sisters, you will face all kinds of trouble. When you do, think of it as pure joy. Your faith will be put to the test. You know that when that happens it will produce in you the strength to continue.

JAMES 1:2–3

find them? That's where the kimberlite comes in. Geologists believe that at one time molten kimberlite—carrying precious diamonds—exploded to the surface of the earth in volcanoes. As the kimberlite cooled, it formed mountains on top of the earth, and upside-down funnel-shaped pipes underground. Over many years, water wore down the kimberlite mountains. Diamonds were carried away in streams and rivers such as the one where Erasmus Jacobs found his pretty pebble. But once gem seekers figured out the connection between diamonds and kimberlite, they extended their search to any area where kimberlite exists. This includes the underground pipes that once

Graphite (GRAFF-ite), the soft, gray substance used in pencil lead, is also made of pure carbon. But graphite isn't formed under great pressure and temperatures. It's not even close to being as tough as diamonds, or as beautiful! The carbon atoms that form graphite crystals are bonded together in rings. These rings are joined loosely in layers; when you write or draw with graphite, a layer of graphite atoms is left on the surface of the paper.

The most recognized diamonds are colorless. But diamonds also come in pink, red, blue, green, yellow, and brown.

Grow It!

Diamonds are crystals. To get an idea about how crystals form, grow your own. You'll need

* 2 cups of sugar
* ½ cup of water
* a small pot
* a clear heatproof glass
* a thin piece of cotton string
* a small nail
* a pencil

First tie a knot in one end of the string and poke the small nail through the knot. Tie the other end of the string to the pencil. Lay the pencil across the top of the glass, letting the free end of the string dangle into the glass.

Now pour the sugar and water into the pot and stir it. With the help of an adult, heat the mixture. Continue to stir to help the sugar dissolve. When it comes to a boil, pour the mixture into the glass. Place the glass in an out-of-the-way place where it can't be jostled. Watch for crystals to grow on the string.

Dig Deeper!

* diamonds
* gems, gemstones
* rocks and minerals

brought the kimberlite—and diamonds—to the surface.

The hardness of diamonds, forged of high heat and pressure, is one of the reasons they're so valuable. Long-lasting diamonds dazzle in necklaces, rings, and pins after they're cut and polished. Diamonds that don't measure up to shape, size, color, and quality standards for jewelry are prized for their use in tools that cut, grind, and polish.

Did you know that in some ways we are like diamonds? Sometimes God allows problems to bring extreme heat and pressure into our lives. This is not a fun place to be! But God has purposes for allowing these problems. He knows that the heat and pressure of problems cause us to turn to Him. He knows they develop our trust in Him. Problems also develop **perseverance**. They make us less proud and more humble. When we understand what it feels like to suffer, we can comfort others who are suffering, too.

Perseverance: (Per-seh-VEER-ents) to keep on going, even though you face difficulties or are discouraged

It's normal for each of us to want everything in our lives to be perfect and easy, free of troubles. None of us likes heat and pressure! But when we believe God is using our troubles for our own good, we won't lose hope. And when we see that Jesus suffered far more than we ever could, we are encouraged to keep going. We can let heat and pressure do their work. We can even have joy, knowing that God is turning our faith into sturdy, dazzling diamonds.

Thought to remember:
Troubles aren't bad. They turn me into one of God's diamonds.

Additional verses:
Romans 5:3–5; 2 Corinthians 1:3–5; Hebrews 12:2–3; James 5:11; 1 Peter 1:6–7

In front of you are three small packages wrapped in silver paper and topped with tiny bows. With anticipation you rip the paper off each package to reveal three black velvet boxes. To your delight, each box holds a sparkly colorless gem, about the size of a pea.

Now suppose you're told you can pick one of these gems to keep and that one of them is a diamond. Which one will you choose? This doesn't seem like a very hard choice; after all, these gems are all the same size and each one looks just like the others. Shrugging your shoulders, you reach for a box. . . .

STOP! Stop right there. Are all three sparkly stones diamonds? Maybe, maybe not. How can you be sure the stone you're choosing is the real thing and not a fake? The answer isn't as simple as it seems.

There are lots of look-alikes in the world of gems. In some cases, an inexpensive natural stone passes for a precious gem. An example is a yellow form of quartz that sometimes passes for topaz, an expensive clear, hard gem.

Look-alikes are also man-made. One of the "diamonds" in your boxes could be **synthetic**, a man-made gem created in a lab. Synthetic diamonds, emeralds, rubies, and sapphires are carbon copies of naturally occurring jewels. They're made of the same minerals. And they share the same qualities that **mineralogists** use to identify natural gems. So how do you tell them apart? It's not always easy. Special tests reveal slight differences. Some jewelers depend on probes to give them the straight scoop on diamonds. And, as strange as it may seem, a peek under the microscope reveals that synthetic gems are too perfect. They don't have as many **inclusions**—tiny solids, liquids, or gases trapped inside—as natural gems. Synthetics may also have fine lines and bubbles that give them away to the trained eye.

If the substitute isn't made of the same materials, then it's an **imitation**. **Cubic zirconia** is a convincing diamond look-alike that's popular with people who can't afford genuine gems or synthetics. Imitations can be nothing more than cheap glass or plastic. And sometimes counterfeits are made by pasting two or three different materials

synthetic: (sin-THET-ik)

mineralogist: (min-nuh-RAH-luh-jist) a person who studies minerals

inclusion: (in-CLUE-zhun)

imitation: (im-ih-TAY-shun) something that's a copy

cubic zirconia: (KYU-bik zer-CONE-ee-uh) This fake may look like a diamond, but it doesn't have the same physical properties.

> God's grace has saved you because of your faith in Christ. Your salvation doesn't come from anything you do. It is God's gift. It is not based on anything you have done. No one can brag about earning it.
>
> EPHESIANS 2:8-9

Here are more gems of info:

* The General Electric Company first produced synthetic diamonds on a large scale in the 1950s. Most of these are very small and used for cutting and drilling.

* Natural emeralds are very expensive and have a lot of inclusions. Synthetic emeralds give more people the chance to own these "little pretties."

* In the past few years another diamond look-alike called moissanite (MOY-zun-ite) has become popular. Made of carbon, silicon, and oxygen, this mineral was originally discovered in a meteorite. Very few of these gemstones exist naturally, but synthetics are now produced in laboratories. Moissanites are more brilliant and have more fire than diamonds, plus, they are nearly as hard. These diamond look-alikes are just about as beautiful as diamonds, and they are less expensive, which makes them more attractive to some buyers!

Check It Out!

Visit a jewelry store to see if you can tell the difference between genuine gems and their counterfeits. Ask the jeweler to show you natural diamonds, emeralds, rubies, and sapphires. Ask to see any synthetic stones or any other substitutes they might have. Can you tell the difference? Perhaps the jeweler can give you some clues on being a stone sleuth.

DIG DEEPER!

* gems
* synthetic gems
* imitation gems
* diamond, emerald, ruby, sapphire

together. Called **doublets** and **triplets**, these copies may actually have a layer of real stone in them. **Opals** are often copied in this way. A layer of opal is glued to the top of a cheaper material and covered with quartz to form a triplet.

There are a lot of look-alikes that pass for the real thing in the gem world! Because of synthetics and imitations, there can be a lot of confusion when it comes to telling the difference between true gems and fakes. A stone that's called a ruby, diamond, or emerald may really be an imitation when put to the test. A simple look on the outside isn't always enough to tell a fake from the real thing.

The same is true for Christians. Suppose you have two friends who go to church every week. They read their Bibles and pray every day. When it comes to giving, your friends can't be beat. You've never met anyone as nice as your two friends. And to top it off, they always seem to look out for the needs of others.

On the outside your friends look exactly alike. Both of them say they're Christians. Are they? Maybe, maybe not.

Just as being clear and sparkly don't make a stone a true diamond, going to church, reading the Bible, praying, and being nice don't make you a true Christian, either. A beautiful stone is a diamond only because it has all the same physical characteristics that all diamonds have. In a similar way, a person is a Christian because he has the same life inside him that all Christians have—Jesus' life. This comes only through believing in Jesus, or depending on Him, to save us from our sins. Imitation life comes from trusting in what we do—it's man-made. Real life comes from trusting in what God has already done for us.

We can't see into the hearts of other people; only God can do that. But we want to be sure that when it comes to ourselves we aren't confused about what it means to be the real thing.

doublet: made of two parts

triplet: made of three parts

opal: (OH-pul) stones with fiery colors that shine out from a milky-white or dark background

Thought to remember:
Believing in Jesus makes me a real Christian.

Additional verses:
1 Samuel 16:7; John 1:12–13; 3:16, 36; 5:24; Acts 16:31; Titus 3:4–5; 1 John 5:11–13

35 TURN MOUNTAINS INTO MOLEHILLS

Lace your boots, zip your jacket, and gather up your pack.

We're going on a trek. All aboard for a tour of the mountains of the world!

While we travel to our first stop, let's glance at a special map of the earth. This is no ordinary map. It's a map of plates—not the kind you eat off of, but pieces of the earth's **crust**. Many scientists believe that the earth's crust and the solid layer underneath are divided into plates, or sections, like giant puzzle pieces. These plates "float" on the layer of earth underneath. As they drift very s-l-o-w-l-y, the continents that ride on top are sometimes forced together. Being forced together creates pressure. This pressure is what shaped the mountains on our tour.

First stop, Mount **Everest**, known as the highest of peaks on earth. Whew! It's dizzying up here on this sharp peak where the air is scarce. Everest is part of a long chain of mountains called the **Himalayas** that stretch between India and China in a crooked smile. It's believed that the plate carrying India pushed north, jamming India into the southern part of Asia. The scrunch was so great that the edges of the earth's crust folded into steep wrinkles to form the Himalayas. That's why Mount Everest is called a folded mountain. If you look around, you can see folds and bends in layers of exposed rock.

From the roof of the world, let's travel to mountains a little closer to home: Grand **Teton** of the Teton Range in Wyoming. This mountain is a shrimp compared to Everest, but it's plenty steep and snowy. Sometimes when the earth's plates move, the crust may crack instead of fold, separating the crust into humongous blocks of rock. Then if these blocks slide up, down, or sideways along these cracks—or faults—they form fault-block mountains. If you look at exposed rock in this mountain, you can see that the layers of rock in the crust don't line up. They zig and zag because one block has slid past another.

Let's throw off our jackets for the next stop, because we're going to visit Hawaii! These islands are actually the tips of volcanoes rising from the depths of the sea. What do volcanic mountains have to do with the earth's moving plates? Most volcanoes form where two plates meet. As one plate is crushed beneath the other, it heats up and melts,

---

CRUST: the outermost layer of the earth

Everest: (EH-vuh-rest)

How tall is Mount Everest? Over 29,000 feet above sea level!

Himalayas: (Him-uh-LAY-uhs)

Teton: (TEE-t'on)

The main island in Hawaii is actually taller than Mount Everest. It's over 30,000 feet high if you measure from its base at the ocean floor.

> It is God who arms me with strength and makes my way perfect. He makes my feet like the feet of a deer; He enables me to stand on the heights.
>
> PSALM 18:32–33
> (NIV)

Mountains have a lot of influence in our lives.

* They affect our weather. Warm, moist air cools as it rises up the sides of mountains, causing rain to fall.

* Many rivers begin in mountains.

* Mountains store valuable water in the form of snow.

* Mountains are fun! We enjoy skiing, camping, and climbing in the mountains. Sometimes it's enough just to enjoy their beauty.

TRY IT!

A dish towel can help you understand how mountains fold. Spread the cloth out on a table. Place your hands on the towel, one on each side. Now move your hands toward the middle—and each other. This forms folds in the towel. In a similar way, when the edges of the earth's crust crumple together, they buckle and fold.

DIG DEEPER

* mountains
* geography

turning to magma. As magma escapes through weak spots in the crust, lava pours out to form volcanoes.

Magma is involved in another type of mountain we'll visit, too. Our last stop? The rounded Black Hills of South Dakota. Sometimes magma flows through a crack in the crust and pools beneath the earth's surface, pushing the rocks above it into a bulge. The magma then cools and hardens to form a rocky core. Over the years, the top layers of the bulge wear away, exposing the hardened core. Then, wind and rain sculpt this rock into individual dome mountains.

Perhaps you live in the mountains or next door to them. Even if you don't, you know all about mountains—the mountains of life. Climbing Everest is difficult and exhausting; pains, problems, and challenges in our lives can be as difficult and exhausting, too. Perhaps . . .

* school is a mountain; you always have to spend more time studying than everybody else.
* kids make fun of you because you're a Christian.
* you have a physical problem that sticks around like the snows of a mountain.
* your parents have had money struggles for as long as you remember.
* the sport or instrument you committed to learning is more work than you bargained for.

If you feel as if you can't take one more step up the rocky slopes of life, don't look up at how far you still have to go. Look at Jesus, your strength. Moment by moment, He gives you the sure feet of a deer to make you able to breeze over steep, rocky paths. Climbing with Him turns mountains into molehills. He makes trails seem smooth, straight, and level.

God knows all about the mountain you're climbing. He is with you every inch of the way. No mountain is too tall or rough for Him to overcome. Let Him take you to the heights!

Thought to remember:
Jesus turns mountains into molehills.

Additional verses:
Psalm 18:28–29; Isaiah 40:28–31; Jeremiah 32:17; Luke 3:5–6; Hebrews 12:2

What comes to mind when you hear the word power?

Superman? The jaws of a shark? Your dad?

How about an earthquake? Have you ever felt its power?

Imagine this: You're standing in your kitchen. The floor suddenly starts to jiggle, and the room sways back and forth. Plates and glasses clink, light fixtures rattle, books fall from their shelves. You try to run, but you're knocked off your feet. Within minutes the earthquake crumbles buildings; causes fires, floods, and landslides; and cracks the ground.

To understand earthquakes, think pressure. As you already know, geologists believe the earth's crust is made of hard plates that fit together like giant puzzle pieces. These plates "float" on top of a softer mantle layer. As they move, their edges can jam together, move apart, or grind against each other. Where they jam together or grind against each other, pressure builds. Suddenly the crust breaks or shifts. Energy is released in the form of shock waves that surge through the crust and shake the ground.

When earthquakes happen on the ocean floor, the sudden jolt sends a strong pulse through the sea. This creates long, low waves that race across deep water at speeds of up to six hundred miles per hour. As a wave nears the gradually sloping shore, it piles up on itself, turning into a giant wave that's more like a wall of water. This giant wave that hits land is called a **tsunami**. Some tsunamis may rise as high as a hundred feet before crashing onto land. Anything in its path drowns or is sucked back to sea.

Maybe the word *power* also made you think of volcanoes. Like earthquakes, most of them take place where plates meet or spread apart. They're also the result of pressure. Melted rock—or magma—and gases collect under the earth's surface. If the magma is thin and runny, gases can escape pretty easily. It can escape in lava flows through weak spots in the crust. But if the magma is thick and sticky, gases can't

Most earthquakes and volcanoes occur along the Ring of Fire, a belt that circles the Pacific Ocean.

tsunami: (tsoo-NAH-me) comes from Japanese words that mean "harbor" and "wave"

Think about trying to control an earthquake or volcano. Impossible! But God has the ultimate power; He can do whatever He wants. He's sovereign (SAHV-ur-in).

> I pray also that the eyes of your heart may be enlightened in order that you may know . . . His incomparably great power for us who believe. That power is like the working of His mighty strength, which He exerted in Christ when He raised Him from the dead. . . .
>
> EPHESIANS
> 1:18a, 19–20 (NIV)

Volcanoes aren't all bad.

* They build mountains and islands.
* Ash from volcanoes improves soil.
* The rock that forms when lava cools is used to build roads.
* Pumice—a lightweight gray volcanic rock—smoothes, polishes, and scrubs. You may have felt this gritty substance if you've ever used heavy-duty hand cleaners.

Try It!

To see the power of pressure that causes earthquakes and volcanoes, all you need is a bottle of soda. (Ask your parents for help with this activity!) First, go outside to a grassy area. Unscrew the cap and pour out a small amount of the soda. Hold your thumb over the top of the bottle and shake it. Set the bottle on the ground at arm's length. Remove your thumb. What happens when pressure builds inside the container?

Make It!

Make your own volcano. You will need

* an empty plastic bottle
* ⅓ cup baking soda
* one cup vinegar
* red food coloring
* a squeeze of liquid dishwashing detergent
* a mound of dirt or sand

Pour the baking soda into the bottle. Bury the bottle in the dirt or sand, leaving the very top uncovered. Mix the vinegar, food coloring, and detergent in a glass or jar. Pour this mixture into the bottle and watch out for the volcano!

DIG DEEPER!

* earthquake
* tsunami
* volcano
* Mount Saint Helens

escape very easily. Pressure builds until lava, ash, steam, rocks, and gases blast through the crust in fiery fountains.

When Mount Saint Helens in Washington State blew its top in 1980, steam and ash exploded miles into the heavens. Clouds of ash choked the sky more than three hundred miles away. Hot hurricane-force winds scorched trees eighteen miles away.

Maybe the word *power* also made you think of God. As amazing and frightening as the power of earthquakes, tsunamis, and volcanoes can be, they're nothing next to God's power. In fact, nothing compares to the power it took for God to raise Jesus from the dead after He paid for our sins.

God uses His power for our benefit. It's a good thing, because compared to Him we're very weak. We see and understand our own weakness when we struggle with family, friends, and school. Sometimes we even struggle with living from day to day. But God doesn't think that being weak is bad. In a way, He made us like the volcano. It's through weak spots in the crust that the power of the volcano is released. It's through our weak spots that God's super power is released.

When you turn to Jesus in your weakness, His life in you is the power to live a full and satisfying life. He is the super power that allows you to be a super kid for Him.

Thought to remember:

God's super power allows me to be a super kid.

Additional verses:

Daniel 4:35; 2 Corinthians 4:7; 12:9; Ephesians 3:20; 2 Peter 1:3a

One drop of rain isn't very powerful.

Neither is a whisper of wind. But when the earth is hammered by a skyful of rain-drops, or wild winds whip the ground, the story changes. Rain and wind are two powerful tools that sculpt our surroundings.

The sculpting goes on all the time. Rocks are broken down—or weathered—by water, wind, plants, and animals. Some of the same forces that loosen the bits of rock then lift and carry them away. This is called **erosion**. Here's how it works:

erosion:
(ih-ROW-zhun)

A trickle of water from a rainstorm or melting snow cuts a groove in the soil. If the trickle turns into a creek, larger rocks and soil particles are scraped away. If the creek grows into a river, then wide, deep channels are carved through valleys. Over many years, a large river can sculpt gorges as large as the Grand Canyon.

Wave power is another way water shapes the earth. Day in and day out, waves wash sand to shore and carry it out again, building up beaches or caus-ing them to shrink. The constant pounding of waves also chisels steep sea cliffs into rocks. Then as waves carve out the bases of these cliffs, sea caves form. Eventually, waves etch all the way through sea caves to create arches. And when the tops of the arches erode, only tall stumps of rock remain.

> **Don't worry about anything.**
>
> PHILIPPIANS 4:6a

Dry particles are easier to pick up than moist particles, because they don't stick together.

While water is busy sculpting, so is the wind. Dry particles of soil are light enough to be lifted by wind and whisked far, far away. Most often, heavier grains simply roll and bounce along the ground.

Dunes form in deserts and near shores where wind packs a punch and the soil is dry and unprotected.

Perhaps you've had the chance to jump and somersault on sand dunes—mountains made of sand. A dune begins when wind runs into an obstacle such as a rock or plant. The obstacle slows the current of wind, causing it to drop its load of sand. As sand col-lects around the object, it blocks more wind. More sand piles up. Eventually the object is buried by a mountain of sand.

Some of the results of erosion are fun—we enjoy playing on beaches and sand dunes sculpted by waves and winds. But sometimes erosion causes problems. Sometimes it gets out of hand. Normally, a network of plant roots helps hold soil particles together. But if too many trees are removed or animals are allowed to overgraze, the roots van-ish. The soil is left naked; wind can pick it up and water can wash it away.

Ice is another tool of erosion. In some places snow sticks around all year. As snowflakes collect year after year, layers build up. Eventually, the top layers of snow crush the lower layers. The snowflakes become grainy. More pressure turns them into ice. This body of ice—called a **glacier** (GLAY-shur)—can become so large and heavy it begins to flow downhill. Glaciers scrub the landscape, moving rocks and boulders. They widen valleys. They also scoop out areas that eventually turn into lakes.

ExpLore It!

To explore the power of water and wind, all you need is a garden hose, water, soil, and a shallow box. Shovel soil into a shallow box. If the soil is moist, let it dry out. When it's dry, gently blow on the soil. Then take a deep breath and blow harder. What happens to the soil each time?

Now turn on the water so that a trickle flows from the hose to the soil. Turn up the water. How does the amount of water affect erosion?

List It!

Our worries come in all sizes. They may be small: *What if no one likes my haircut?* They may be large: *What if Mom and Dad die?* Whether small or large, they all erode our peace. Grab a pencil and paper and find a quiet corner. Make a list of everything you worry about. When your list is done, show it to God. Tell Him all about your worries. Thank Him for being your Father and taking care of you.

DIG DEEPER!

* erosion
* geography
* water
* wind
* sand dunes
* glaciers

Farming methods can also cause erosion to get out of control. This happens when fields are plowed in straight lines, allowing water to rush along the rows. Some crops such as corn don't completely cover the ground, leaving strips of soil exposed to wind and water. The result? Deep gullies gouge the land, making it useless for farming.

What are some solutions? Farmers alternate crops. They plant crops that completely cover the ground next to sections of corn. When plowing, they follow the curves of the land to slow the flow of water. Farmers also leave dead plants in the soil to hold soil particles together and return important vitamins and minerals to the earth.

Wind and water are tools of erosion that naturally sculpt the earth. But when they get out of control, they scar the land and steal precious soil. Erosion is a picture of what happens in our lives when we worry. Here's how it happens: It's natural for us to care about our lives and have concern for others. But sometimes care turns into worry. Before we know it, a small trickle of worry can turn into a raging river. That river can cut the Grand Canyon through the peace and rest in our hearts! We become nervous. We can't think straight. Even our health is affected. So much time is spent worrying about what *might* take place that we miss out on living right now.

What's the solution? God tells us not to worry about *anything* (see Philippians 4:6). Instead of focusing on our problems, He wants us to come to Him with them. Most of the things we worry about never come true. But even if one of them does, God assures us He'll be right here with us. His sweet peace and rest can replace our greatest fears and worries.

Why waste your life being anxious? Worry can't change a thing. Instead, tell your heavenly Father what's troubling you. Trust Him to return peace to your heart.

Thought to remember:
Turn to God with every worry.

Additional verses:
Matthew 6:25–34; John 14:27; Philippians 4:6–7

Sand is all over the place. We like to play in it, lie on it, and build sand castles with it. But have you ever stopped to take a good look at sand? A really good close-to-your-nose look? Grab a swimsuit, shovel, and magnifying glass. We're going to poke around in the sand.

First stop, sand dunes. What does this tan sand look like through a magnifying glass? That's right—tiny, tiny rocks! That gives us a clue about where sand comes from. Large parent rocks, especially quartz, are the source for most sand. How do they get to be this size? Rocks at the earth's surface are broken into smaller and smaller bits through a process called *weathering*. What causes weathering?

Sand grains are smaller than gravel, but bigger than particles that make mud.

Water does. Rain, waves, and rivers scrub away tiny particles of rock. Stones carried by rivers and waves smash against each other and break apart. Water also sneaks inside the cracks in rocks. When water freezes, it expands and acts like a wedge, pushing the crack apart. A rock can freeze and thaw and freeze and thaw until it crumbles.

Air and water can create chemical changes in rocks that cause them to break into pieces, too.

Water is just one tool of weathering. Wind scours rocks, too. It sandblasts with the particles it carries. Plant roots and burrowing animals can even split rocks. Hot and cold temperatures also cause them to expand and contract—and eventually crack.

Our next stop is a stretch of bright white sand on a tropical beach. What do you notice about these white grains? These particles look like itty-bitty bits of shell. That gives us a clue about where this sand comes from. The fragile shells of ocean animals are

fragment: (FRAG-ment) a small piece

broken into **fragments** as waves crash them onto the beach, rocks, and each other. The pinkish red particles are the remains of coral pieces, also pounded by waves.

Last stop, Hawaii. This beach isn't blond or white. It's black! Can you guess where black sand comes from? Here's a clue: Hawaii has active volcanoes. Black lava flows to the ocean and instantly cools, shattering into shiny black crumbs.

How do sand particles end up on beaches, in deserts, and in sand dunes? By some of the same forces that form them to begin with. Rivers carry sand to the ocean.

> Can you fathom the mysteries of God? Can you probe the limits of the Almighty? They are higher than the heavens. . . . They are deeper than the depths of the grave. . . . Their measure is longer than the earth and wider than the sea.
>
> JOB 11:7–9 (NIV)

Here are more sand facts:

★ In addition to tan, black, and white, sand can be red or green or a mixture of the two. Some sand looks like salt and pepper.

★ There are more uses for sand than making sand castles! It's used to make glass and sandpaper, and it's also mixed with cement to make concrete.

★ Glaciers—huge bodies of ice that flow slowly over land—also move sand.

Discover It!

To get an idea about the incredible number of sand grains on this earth, all you need is a handful of sand, a piece of dark paper, a sharp pencil, and your counting skills.

First, find some dry sand. Scoop up a handful of sand and pile it on the paper. Using the pencil to separate grains, count them. Did you finish counting all the sand in the pile?

Think about how many handfuls of sand there must be in the world. Yet that number is limited. Does this help you see how amazing our God is?

Draw It!

Make a sand painting. Dye small amounts of sand with food coloring; let the sand dry. Next draw a simple picture on a piece of cardboard. Spread glue over a small area and sprinkle the color of sand you want on that section. Continue to glue sand to your drawing until you've filled in the whole picture.

DIG DEEPER!

★ sand
★ beaches
★ sand dunes
★ deserts
★ rocks, weathering

Ocean waves whisk sand onto beaches. Wind blows clouds of these salt-sized particles into towering mounds called sand dunes.

Now scoop up a handful of sand and let it sift through your fingers. How many grains do you think passed through your fingers? Thousands? Perhaps millions? How many handfuls of sand are on this beach? In all the beaches in the world, plus all the deserts, sand dunes, rivers, and lakes?

That's a lot of sand—a number we can't begin to grasp! But even though the number of sand grains is a *huge*, unthinkable number, that number is limited. Another way to say this is that there is a **finite** number of sand grains on earth. Everything—whether on earth or reaching to the skies—is finite.

finite: (FY-nite) limited

But God is not.

He is unlimited—or **infinite**—in every way. There are no limits to God's power, His understanding, His faithfulness, His goodness . . . His amazing love.

infinite: (IN-fih-nit) without limit

Knowing that God is infinite in all His ways fills our hearts with **awe**; it humbles us. It comforts and encourages us. We can be sure that when God says He is able, He can't come up short, as people here on earth do.

awe: (AW) worship, respect, wonder, and fear all rolled into one

And then when we realize that the unlimited God wants to know us and live inside us—even though we're very limited—it makes us stop in amazement. Can we be *that* special? We can't begin to understand His care for us. Our hearts are overwhelmed with wonder and gratefulness.

The next time you build a sand castle or visit sand dunes, scoop up a handful of sand. Try to count the number of grains. Remember that sand gives us a clue to help us understand God. There's nothing on earth that compares with our unlimited God. Believing that can change your life.

Thought to remember:
God has no limits. He is infinite!

Additional verses:
Psalm 136:1–3; 145:3, 9; 147:5; Isaiah 40:28–31; Romans 11:33–36 (NIV)

I magine you're on a hike, traveling deep into thick forests on a narrow trail. Scattered patterns of late-afternoon light flicker on the path. A metallic buzz of insects drowns out other sounds. The hot, moist air is heavy with smells of plants and black soil.

At the crossing of a small river comes a chance to stop and wipe trickles of sweat from your cheeks. Letting your pack slide to the ground, you consider the safest way across these bubbly waters. Three easy steps over the sandy shore, two giant steps onto rounded rocks sticking above the water, and you're on the other side. You decide to try it without your pack.

There's no problem making it from the bank to the first rock. The step from rock to rock takes more of a leap. So does the final gap from rock to shore, but you land safely on the other side . . . and sink to your ankles.

Before you know it, the mushy sand is up to your knees. This is no ordinary sand. It's quicksand. Panicking, you thrash your arms and try to lift your legs. The sand is up to your waist now and rising. You're hopelessly stuck in the muck. "Help! Somebody help!" you scream. No one answers. What are you going to do?

> So faith comes from hearing the message. And the message that is heard is the word of Christ.
>
> ROMANS 10:17

Stop! Stop struggling and listen to some simple facts about the sand that swallows.

There's nothing unusual about the ingredients that make up quicksand—it's simply sand and water. What's unusual is how they're mixed together. As you know, usually when you walk on wet sand, it presses together, or **compacts**, becoming hard and firm. But it's a different story when water flows up from *underneath* the sand and a cushion of water surrounds each grain. As a result the grains are slightly separated. They can't settle or press together—and they can't support heavy weight.

The bad news is, struggling and thrashing about in quicksand only make you sink deeper. Large animals such as horses, cattle, and deer usually struggle when they step into the sand that swallows. That's why they sink and drown.

The good news is, if you stop struggling, you'll float. And if you stretch your arms out to the side, your weight will spread out over the surface and you'll float even better. Then with extra-slow swimming movements of hands and arms, you can float your

compact:
(Kum-PAKT)

Why do we float on quicksand? Because it's denser than we are. That means quicksand has more matter in a certain amount of space than we do.

95

More curious quicksand facts:

* The word *quick* means to move, flow, or shift. Can you see how these words describe quicksand?

* Quicksand behaves more like a liquid than a solid.

* Where do quicksand traps form? Near swamps and rivers, as well as in sand dunes by the ocean.

* Underground water for quicksand often comes from springs.

* Even though very few people actually die in quicksand, it still needs to be taken seriously!

Make It!

How does quicksand feel? See for yourself. Pour two or three cups of sand into a container. Add water until it covers the sand. Now scoop some of the wet sand into your hand, keeping it underwater. Does it feel mushy? The cushion of water between the grains of sand keeps them from pressing against one another.

Write It!

Below are the verses Romans 8:38–39. Fill the blanks in with your problems.

I am absolutely sure that not even death or life can separate us from God's love. Not even _____ or _____, _____ or _____, or _____ can do that. Not even _____, or anything else in all creation can do that. Nothing at all can ever separate us from God's love because of what Christ Jesus our Lord has done.

DIG DEEPER!

* quicksand
* geography

way to safety!

Just as we can get stuck in quicksand, we can also get stuck in the quicksand of doubt. Here's how it can happen: Your parents are so busy they don't have much time for you. You don't like your new class at school. Grandpa—who used to be your best friend—has Alzheimer's and doesn't even recognize you. On top of all that, your dog has also grown old; yesterday you overheard your parents' whispers about putting him to sleep. You panic and struggle. You're so overwhelmed, all you can think about are these problems. Doubts begin to spin through your head and heart: *God's not really here. He can't take care of me. He doesn't really love me—all this wouldn't be happening if He did. He isn't on my side and doesn't hear my prayers. God must be mad at me. Why doesn't He make all these problems go away? I must have done something wrong.*

The bad news is, with each doubt you sink a little deeper, until it seems as if you'll drown. What are you going to do?

Stop! Stop struggling and listen to God. He says: "I know you're having a hard time. Here. Rest your head on my shoulder. Let me hold you in the safety of my strong hands. Don't be scared or discouraged. I love you no matter what. I'm always with you—I'm here with you now, going through these problems with you. I am on your side" (see Psalm 139:1–5; Isaiah 49:16; John 10:29; Romans 8:31, 38–39).

The good news is, as you listen to God and believe Him, you'll relax and stop sinking. You'll float on top of the quicksand of doubt. Before you know it, you'll be safe on the shores of hope and peace.

Thought to remember:

Believing God gives me hope and peace.

Additional verses:

Proverbs 3:5; Jeremiah 29:11 (NIV); Matthew 14:25–32; Hebrews 11:1; Jude 1:24 (NIV)

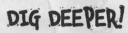

40 The Potter and the Clay

The potter cradles the lump of gray clay in his hands.

He enjoys the familiar way it feels, cool and moist. Turning it over and over in his hands, he considers the steps needed to bring shape to this formless mass. Then he gently smoothes it with his thumbs. This clay has come a long, long way; now it's his to shape into a work of art.

knead: (NEED) the process potters use to prepare clay

At a wood table, the potter rests his hands on the mound. First he will **knead** the clay. The potter pushes down and forward with the palms and heels of his hands. The stiff mass flattens under the pressure. Then he rocks it back toward the edge of the table, twisting the clay slightly before pushing again. Over and over, the potter presses, rocks, and twists to mix the clay and work out air bubbles. The wise potter knows kneading will spread water evenly throughout the clay to make it easier to mold and hold its shape.

O Lord, you are our Father. We are the clay, you are the potter; we are all the work of your hand.

ISAIAH 64:8 (NIV)

Bubbles could cause his piece of art to crack or explode under high temperatures.

Now the shaping begins. He places the clay at the middle of his potter's wheel and turns on the wheel. It begins to spin. Cupping one hand on the side and one on top, the potter presses the turning clay until it molds into a dome, even all around.

Then, with firm pressure, he pushes his thumb into the center of the spinning clay to form a hollow. Holding his thumb steady, the potter increases the pressure on the inside, widening the space. Next he squeezes the walls between his fingers and thumb, pulling up on the walls. The walls slowly grow taller and thinner. When the

fire: to bake clay at high temperatures. This removes water to harden it.

sides of the vase are the right thickness and height, the potter reaches inside with his hand. Pressing on the inside with his fingertips and on the outside with his bent finger, he shapes a bulge at the middle and above that, a neck. At last the potter trims and smoothes his work of art. Satisfied, he lifts the vase and sets it on a shelf.

kiln: (KIHLN or KIHL) the special oven used to fire clay

The vase remains on the shelf until hard and dry. But the potter isn't finished yet. Water could still soften and ruin the vase. It needs to be baked—or **fired**—at high temperatures to set its shape permanently. The potter packs the vase in a special oven called a **kiln**. The temperature inside the kiln rises slowly until it reaches nearly two thousand degrees. Nearly twenty-four hours later, the vase is allowed to cool. Now it

- Clay particles are so small, they can't be seen by the naked eye.

- The tiny particles in a lump of clay used to be particles in rocks. Constant scrubbings by wind, water, and ice freed the tiny grains. Currents of wind and water then carried the grains far and wide, until they settled at the mouths of rivers or quiet lake bottoms.

- The main ingredients in pottery clays are the minerals silica (SIL-ih-kuh) and alumina (uh-LOO-mih-nuh), plus water.

- A potter can easily push, pull, stretch, and mold clay because water mixed in with the tiny clay particles makes it "plastic."

- Firing clay drives out water and permanently hardens the pottery.

Make It!

In this activity you get to be the potter. All you need is some clay, a board or plastic tablecloth to work on, and your imagination. (You can substitute Sculpy or modeling clay if you can't find clay used for pottery.) Pat, pinch, roll, squeeze, or flatten clay to shape pots, animals, tiles, or anything else you dream up!

DIG DEEPER!

- clay
- ceramics
- pottery

will be coated with glaze and fired again. Only then will the vase be ready for the potter's use.

Did you know God calls himself the Potter, and He compares us to clay? Can you think of some reasons why?

Perhaps one reason is, God treats us like clay to shape our faith into works of art for Him. Sometimes He allows situations in our lives that we're not comfortable with. During these times it feels as if God is pushing, pulling, stretching, and molding us—and it hurts! It may even feel as if He has locked us inside a burning hot kiln!

Perhaps another reason is that He wants us to be just like clay as He lovingly shapes us. What does the lump of clay do while the potter kneads, shapes, trims, and fires it? Nothing at all! It simply accepts the pressure and stretching that shape it into a work of art.

Sometimes we don't act like clay, though.

As God works the air bubbles out of our lives, sometimes we think He doesn't love us. We throw temper tantrums when He pulls, presses, and squeezes us into shape. When He sets us on a shelf, we pout and accuse Him of forgetting about us. While being fired in a kiln, we shout that we don't want any more heat!

But the Potter's hands are loving hands. They're skillful hands that always know what's best. Believing the wise Potter knows what He's doing helps us to trust Him, no matter what situation we find ourselves in. Then we can stop struggling against Him. In accepting His work in our lives, we find peace.

Thought to remember:

I am like clay in my Father's loving hands.

Additional verses:

Isaiah 29:16; 45:9; Romans 9:20–21;
1 Corinthians 6:19–20; 1 Peter 1:6–7; 5:6–7

41 THE SURPRISE INSIDE

Do you like fun surprises? Everybody does! We can't wait to tear into packages that come in the mail. We dig around for the prizes sealed inside cereal boxes. We bite into chocolates hoping to find our favorite fillings hidden within.

Believe it or not, there are fun surprises inside rocks, too. Rocks with secrets at the center are called **geodes**.

geode: (JEE-ode) comes from a Greek word that means "earthlike"

If you came across a geode lying in the dirt, you might just walk on by. That's because at first glance geodes don't look like much more than balls of rock. There's nothing pretty about them; they're mostly round, plain boring brown, and kind of lumpy. But that's the outside. If you crack one open, you might be startled to discover amazing treasures inside. The hearts of geodes are often hollow and lined with glittering crystals and rings of unusual colors.

For geodes to form, you've got to have rocks with hollow centers. How could these come about? Scientists aren't quite sure, but they do have some ideas. Some geodes are made out of molten rock. Lava could easily have hardened around trapped gas bubbles to shape rocks with spaces inside.

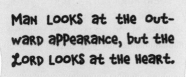

MAN LOOKS AT THE OUT-WARD APPEARANCE, but tHE LORD LOOKS AT tHE HEART.

1 SAMUEL 16:7b
(NIV)

But other geodes are found in sedimentary rocks. Figuring out how geodes develop out of layers of mud is a bit trickier. Scientists think minerals may have settled around decaying plants and animals to create rocks with pockets. Then, chemical changes in the minerals could have caused these sedimentary shells to turn into hard outer coverings that wouldn't weather away.

Once hollow rocks have formed, how do beautiful bands of colors and glittering crystals blossom in the centers? Perhaps water and minerals were trapped in the spaces. Or perhaps water carrying dissolved minerals seeped into the shells. As the water evaporated from the hearts of geodes, minerals that were left behind grew into rings of stone and sparkling clear, white, or purple crystals.

To discover more about Sedimentary ROCKS, turn to "Solid as a Rock" on Page 79.

Geodes are plain on the outside, but beautiful on the inside. In our world of movie stars and supermodels, we tend to turn away from people who are plain on the outside. Some of us go to a lot of trouble trying to look like models ourselves.

There's nothing wrong with outward beauty or taking care of our bodies—after all,

Here are more sparkly geode facts to add to your collection:

* Geodes range in size from marbles to softballs to basketballs—and bigger. They may also be egg-shaped and oblong.

* Sometimes the heart of a geode may be filled with oil, water, sand, or a disappointing muddy sludge.

* To open a geode without breaking the crystals, carve a line around its middle. Continue to trace the line until it deepens enough for the rock to split in two. Geodes can also be cut open with a rock saw.

Check It Out!

Ask your parents to take you to a rock shop where you can examine geodes for yourself. Can you see the layers that form the outer shell, inner colors, and crystals? You may also be able to buy unopened geodes to take home so you can discover the surprises inside for yourself.

DIG DEEPER!

* geodes
* rocks

God is pleased with how He made us. But if outward beauty were important to God, Jesus would have had an attractive body himself. He didn't. Jesus was like a geode, plain on the outside but astonishingly beautiful on the inside.

Because of the world we live in, it's important to remember God's view on beauty. He doesn't want us to focus on our outward appearance. He wants us to focus on Him. True beauty—inner beauty—comes from following God, from being convinced of His love, from letting His life flow out to others.

If you know someone who isn't very attractive, think geode. Take time to get to know him or her. You may be surprised to find there's a prize inside. Beyond a big nose, imperfect skin, or a pudgy body could be a wonderful heart.

And if you're worried about how you look, think geode. Remember, the beauty of your heart is what counts. Focus on God, not yourself; let His life shine through you and you will sparkle from the inside out!

Thought to remember:
Inner beauty is what counts.

Additional verses:
Genesis 1:26, 31a; Psalm 139:13–14; Proverbs 31:30; Ecclesiastes 3:11a; Isaiah 53:2–3; 55:8

42 Salt Secrets

You're sitting in the movie theater, waiting for the film to begin. Dipping into a cardboard bucket for a fistful of crunchy, buttery, melt-in-your-mouth popcorn, you take your first bite. Right away you notice something's wrong. Something's missing. This popcorn tastes blah. What's the deal?

There isn't any salt!

Not only do we sprinkle table salt on popcorn, but the tiny white grains also add pizzazz to a lot of our favorite junk foods. French fries, crackers, pretzels, and chips just don't taste the same without it. And if we do a little detective work, we'll discover that salt is a popular ingredient in a lot of foods. Even foods that satisfy a sweet tooth are made with salt!

Our enjoyment of table salt isn't new. If we peek back in history, we'll see that at one time salt was so important it was as valuable as gold. It was exchanged for slaves. Cities sprung up wherever it was produced, and trade routes opened to transport it. Some governments even put a tax on this seasoning.

> **You are the salt of the earth.**
>
> MATTHEW 5:13a

Adding flavor to foods wasn't the only reason salt was precious, though. Long ago people didn't have freezers, so they depended on this fine white stuff to **preserve** meat. Salt draws moisture out of foods and dries them. This can stop meat from spoiling for several months.

Preserve:
(pre-ZERV)
to keep from
spoiling

Health was another reason salt was so important. This tiny crystal is necessary for healthy blood and cells, but it is lost through sweat and tears. So salt needs to be replaced. In the past people also used salt as a drug.

Today salt may not be used to cure coughs or toothaches, but it's still used for more than a treat for our taste buds. Salt is used to prepare meats, nuts, pickles, cheeses, and many other foods. It's used to make other chemicals, melt ice on streets and sidewalks, tan leather, and make dyes. And if you've ever made ice cream, then you know that salt is used in ice-cream freezers, too.

These are only a sprinkling of modern uses for this seasoning!

Jesus pointed out another use for salt. He compared His followers to this tangy ingredient so important to everyday life. He said, "You are the salt of the earth." Why do you think Jesus said that?

One reason might have to do with using salt to keep food from spoiling. As we fol-

Table salt is a combination of two elements, sodium and chlorine. Sodium is a soft, silvery metal. Chlorine is a yellowish green gas. Sodium or chlorine would poison you if you ate either one by itself. But once they're combined chemically, they form the tiny cube-shaped crystals necessary for a healthy body.

Salt isn't as valuable as gold today because most countries now produce their own salt. In the past salt was harvested from seawater. Seawater was allowed to evaporate, and the salt that was left behind was collected. This method is still used today. But in the mid-1800s many salt mines opened around the world to harvest this seasoning from the inside of the earth.

FiND It!

Be a salt sleuth. Check out ingredient lists on the labels of jars, cans, boxes, and bags in your cupboards and refrigerator. Discover how often salt is used. Make a list of foods containing salt.

In past centuries people struggled to get enough salt because it wasn't as plentiful as today. But now salt is present in so many foods, doctors caution us to be careful not to eat too much. Too much salt can be hard on your heart and kidneys.

DIG DEEPER!

* salt, table salt
* sodium
* chorine

low Jesus, God uses our lives to keep sin from spreading on this earth. He uses us to show others their need for God.

Salt is used to preserve food, but it's also used as a flavoring to make food taste better. As followers of Jesus with His Spirit living inside us, we are flavoring, or seasoning, to this world. When His love is sprinkled through us, the lives of people around us are touched. Add joy, peace, patience, kindness, goodness, faithfulness, gentleness, and self-control, and you can see why our lives can bring the flavor of God to this world.

God uses our lives to make people hungry and thirsty for Him, too. When we eat a little salt we want more. In a similar way, people who come in contact with Jesus' love and mercy through us also want more. Then, just as salt makes us thirsty, they're thirsty for Jesus. They go away searching for Him, the Living Water, the only one who can quench the thirst of their hearts.

If you belong to Jesus, remember: You are the salt of the earth. God will use you in the lives of others.

Thought to remember:
I am the salt of the earth.

Additional verses:
John 7:37; 2 Corinthians 3:3; 5:20;
Galatians 5:22–23 (NIV); Ephesians 2:10

If you've ever sat in a dinky boat out in the middle of the ocean, then you know the feeling. Except for sky, miles of blue-green water stretch out around you with no end in sight. The water slaps lazily against the side of the boat, and you're reminded that only a few inches of wood separate you from the tons and tons of water below. The ocean suddenly feels overwhelmingly huge. And suddenly you feel very, very small.

How big is the ocean? BIG! Nearly three-fourths of the earth is covered by ocean waters. That's why our planet looks blue from space. Almost all of the earth's water is stored in the world's seas. Only a tiny amount is found in rivers, lakes, and ice.

The earth's oceans are all part of one connected body of water, the world ocean. But the continents divide the world ocean into three main sections we call the Pacific, Atlantic, and Indian Oceans. The Pacific Ocean is the largest. This body of water is so huge, it accounts for about half of the earth's ocean area. It's so enormous that all seven continents could fit into the Pacific and there would still be room for another hunk of land as big as Asia. At its widest point near the equator, the Pacific Ocean is a whopping 15,000 miles wide. From its northern boundaries to the shores of Antarctica in the south, it spans about 9,600 miles.

The Atlantic Ocean covers about half the area of the Pacific. Some scientists include the Arctic Ocean with the Atlantic, making it even bigger. The Indian Ocean is less than half the size of the Pacific. Put these three large bodies of water together, and you can see why the world ocean seems as if it stretches on without end.

The world ocean is gigantic as it spreads over the earth's surface. But it's also deep. How deep? On average, there are more than two miles of water from the ocean surface to the bottom. But the deepest parts are found in trenches, narrow valleys found near the edges of continents. The deepest of the deep known to man is the **Mariana** Trench in the Pacific Ocean. To reach the bottom of the Mariana Trench, you'd have to descend nearly seven miles.

Some scientists divide the world ocean into five parts: the Pacific, Atlantic, Indian, Arctic, and Antarctic Oceans. Other scientists include the Antarctic with the Pacific Ocean and the Arctic with the Atlantic.

Mariana: (mare-ee-ANN-uh)

> May you have power with all God's people to understand Christ's love. May you know how wide and long and high and deep it is. And may you know his love, even though it can't be known completely.
>
> EPHESIANS 3:18–19

Here are more awesome ocean facts:

* The ocean floor is made of broad plains with a long chain of mountains, the midocean ridge, running through the middle. Single volcanic mountains are also scattered here and there.

* The ocean deeps may be like tropical rain forests—packed with huge numbers of different kinds of animals.

* Many creatures of the deep live off of "marine snow," bits of plants and animals that fall from above.

* The ocean is full of treasures helpful to humans. Fish, crab, shrimp, oyster, lobster, and seaweed are harvested for food. Oil and gas found under the ocean floor provide energy. Minerals are mined from water and the ocean floor. Some drugs have also been produced from marine plants and animals.

As wide and long and deep as the world ocean is, you can imagine that it holds a massive amount of water. That's an understatement! The number of gallons in the ocean is a number far greater than our minds can comprehend.

The world ocean is so amazingly huge, it's hard to grasp just how wide and long and deep it is! Sometimes it's hard for us to grasp how great Jesus' love is, too. In the New Testament the apostle Paul prays that we'll be able to grasp how wide and long and high and deep the love of Jesus is for us . . . that we'll be able to know this love that's so great we could never completely take it all in.

How great is His love? He fills each of our lives with more blessings than there are drops of water in the ocean. Here are only a few:

* God is patient and merciful with us.

* God the Father sent us a love letter in the form of His Son, Jesus.

* God the Son has scars in His hands, feet, and side to prove His love.

* God holds our hands.

* God the Father holds us in the safety of His hand.

* God the Father turned His back on Jesus, who carried our sins.

* God will *never* turn His back on us.

* God always forgives.

* God the Father gives us His Spirit, the Helper.

* God comforts us.

* God gave the Word—the Bible—to teach us.

* God speaks to us through the Word, Jesus.

* God freckles the sky with stars and knows the name of every single one.

* God knows our names.

* God reveals himself to us.

* God lets us in on the secrets of how the world works.

* God doesn't forget that we're human. Food, a warm bath, a good night's sleep . . . are all gifts of His love.

Our list could go on and on and on. . . .

God's love is far wider than the ocean, far deeper than the sea. His love is the foundation of our lives. It cuts through any problem we could have on this earth. How do our hearts respond to this?

There are no words great enough to express our gratitude to Him. In silence our hearts kneel before Him with worship and praise.

Thought to remember:

God's love for me is wider than the ocean, deeper than the sea.

Additional verses:

Deuteronomy 33:12; Psalm 33:5; 90:14; 103:11; 107:8; 108:4; John 21:25; Romans 5:8; James 1:17 (NIV); 1 John 3:1; 4:16

List It!

Grab a pen and some paper. Find a quiet spot to think about every way God shows His love to you. Write down each thought as it comes to mind. Tell God how grateful you are for His love and how much you love Him. As you go through each day, think about the many, many ways—large and small—that God shows His love to you.

DIG DEEPER!

★ oceans

★ Pacific, Atlantic, Indian Oceans

On a clear night, far away from city lights, you can see the Milky Way—a filmy white band stretched across the sky. *What's out there?* you wonder. A telescope reveals bright planets, hosts of stars, and cloudy gatherings of gases and dust. But what's really out there? Are aliens hidden among those stars? Some people think there are.

It thrills some of us to believe life exists on distant planets in distant galaxies. But most likely, it's not much more than a thrill. The more we discover about our universe, the more we see that chances for extraterrestrials are pretty slim. A lot of puzzle pieces have to fit together perfectly for complex life to exist on a planet. So far, only earth seems to have all the pieces to the puzzle. It's no accident that earth, our place in space, is the perfect place for life. Here are a few of the puzzle pieces:

The Milky Way is spiral shaped. This shape is rare. When it formed, the chemicals needed for life also formed. Most galaxies are either oval shaped or irregular, with no particular shape at all.

My God will meet all your needs. He will meet them in keeping with His wonderful riches that come to you because you belong to Christ Jesus.

PHILIPPIANS
4:19

* The position of our sun in an arm of the Milky Way is not too close and not too far from other stars, but just right. If other stars were closer, the earth's orbit would be thrown out of whack. If they were farther away, the chemicals necessary for life would not have formed.

* Our sun is not too big and not too small, but just right. If the sun were bigger, it would burn up too fast. If it were smaller, we'd turn to ice cubes!

* Our sun is not too close and not too far away, but just right. Shrinking the distance between sun and earth would fry us. Not only would we be exposed to more intense heat from the sun, but our planet's rotation time would also decrease. Instead of twenty-four hours, one day would last years, creating temperature extremes that destroy life. It's no mistake we're 93 million miles away from the sun. This distance provides the perfect touch of light to keep temperatures cozy and make our planet sparkle with water—both necessary for life.

mass: the amount
of matter
in an object.

To discover more
about air, turn to
"Inside, Outside,
All Around" on
page 69.

To discover more
about clouds, turn
to "A Cat, a King,
an Angel's Wing"
on page 73.

* The earth is not too big and not too small, but just right. Its **mass** provides the exact amount of gravity needed to hold on to the best mixture of gases for our atmosphere. Our atmosphere makes life possible and protects us from the sun.

* The size of our moon is not too big and not too small, but just right. The moon's perfect size gives us tides. It helps keep the tilt of the earth constant, giving us seasons and variety of life. This variety helps balance the water supply and gases in our atmosphere.

* The earth's oceans are not too big, not too small, but just right. Our large oceans store warmth from the sun. They're a source of clouds to scatter rains over the earth.

* The earth's magnetic field is not too large, not too small, but just right. Scientists believe that the very center, or core, of the earth creates the magnetic field that extends way beyond the atmosphere. This field is a shield that protects us from harmful particles from the sun.

The earth has a fixed amount of substances that are very important to life. As water, oxygen, nitrogen, and carbon are used, they're also recycled, so the earth never runs out. The earth is an amazingly well-balanced planet!

These are a few of many reasons the earth is perfect for life. There's nothing puzzling about why there's no better place in space for us than earth. And while we live here, there's no better place for us than *in Jesus*. He's our perfect place in this world. Why?

Just as the universe, Milky Way, sun, and earth completely supply all the needs of our bodies, Jesus completely supplies all the needs of our hearts. Another way to say this: We're complete in Jesus.

Before we know Jesus, there's something missing from our lives; it's as if a piece of the puzzle of our lives is missing. We can try to complete the puzzle in many ways. Being the smartest person in school, buying a lot of expensive toys, or joining the "in-crowd" are just a few substitutes for the missing piece. There's nothing wrong with being smart, buying toys, or being popular, but the problem is, they don't fit the puzzle! True love, joy, happiness, and satisfaction can only be found in Jesus.

Find It!

When we believe in Jesus, He supplies us with everything we need for our lives. He provides it with His life. Here is a short list of what becomes yours when you find your place in Jesus. Find the words in the puzzle below. Words are forward, backward, up, down, and diagonal.

DIRECTION	JOY	POWER
FREEDOM	LIFE	SELF-CONTROL
GENTLENESS	LOVE	STRENGTH
GRACE	PATIENCE	TRUTH
HOPE	PEACE	WISDOM

```
Z E L P N G E N T L E N E S S F
G W A T R O M H V E X C D E B G
F H T G N E R T S R N E C L D E
I O L E N V E U S E T P H F N C
F P I P O W E R I L L T U C J B
J E O S I R B T A R D A I O L S
P A H S T M A E L D N T R N I L
K L D A C P R N Y Z C Q I T C N
R O M I E E N D Y Q I S E R N P
M V M G R A C E F I L B E O Y M
X E Y P I C S R L F M D I L G U
W T A R D E E E Y M L O V L J B
H B E U L E H A W F R R S C Y K
E D X P D K H Y R M F A I R T S
T Q J O Y Z V L E L A R I P Z E
K J M H E X R S A O D L W M U R
```

The answers are on page 150.

DIG DEEPER!

* earth
* planets
* solar system
* space

Belonging to God puts you in Jesus. Everything you need for a satisfying life is found in Him. He fills up what's missing in our lives. Finding our perfect place in Jesus brings purpose to our lives and gives us a reason to live. In Jesus, the puzzle of our lives is complete. He's our perfect place.

Thought to remember:

Jesus is my perfect place. I am complete in Him.

Additional verses:

Acts 17:28a; Romans 8:32; 1 Corinthians 2:12; Ephesians 1:3; Philippians 1:21a; Colossians 1:19; 2:9–10

Month after month, year after year,
the signs of seasons come and go—
Winter arrives with a sharp wind that bites.
Days are cut short by endless dark nights.
But sooner or later, warmer winds blow.
Spring tiptoes in with the melting of snow.
Brown earth turns green; it awakens from sleep.
Young robins and sparrows in nests cry and cheep.
With the beginning of summer and ending of spring,
the last half of the year is into full swing.
On sunny hot days, bugs take to the skies.
At night there are cricket and frog lullabies.
Then crisp weather brings in the first autumn freeze,
bushes with berries, crunchy brown leaves. . . .
And when the mild days of fall finally end,
the signs of the seasons start over again.

Each of us is familiar with the rhythm of seasons where we live. What are the reasons for seasons? There are basically two: the tilt of the earth and the earth's journey around the sun.

To understand, pretend you're perched out in space where you can watch the earth as it circles, or revolves, around the sun. If you poke an imaginary rod through the top of the earth and out the bottom, you see that the rod doesn't point straight up and down. You'll notice that the earth tilts slightly. This tilt always stays the same.

IN THE NORTHERN HEMISPHERE, THE FIRST DAY OF SPRING FALLS ON MARCH 20, 21, OR 22. THE FIRST DAY OF AUTUMN FALLS ON SEPTEMBER 22 OR 23.

I AM THE LORD. I DO NOT CHANGE.

MALACHI 3:6a

Now watch the tilted earth as it revolves around the sun for a whole year. The tilt affects how much sunlight hits different parts of the earth *at different times of the year.* In winter, the top half—or northern hemisphere—is tilted away from the sun. The sun appears lower in the sky and is up for less time than in the other seasons. The sun's low position and shorter days mean less heat to the top half of the earth. This produces cooler, sometimes icy, winter seasons.

Just as God's kindness, patience, and love are steady, so is His attitude toward sin. God is always pure and perfect. He cannot sin, and He won't allow sin in His presence. But the person who has a change of mind about his or her sin will always find God ready to forgive.

As the earth continues to travel around the sun, you'll notice that in spring neither the north nor south poles are pointed toward the sun. On the first day of spring, the amounts of daytime and nighttime are the same everywhere on earth. The sun is directly overhead at the **equator**. The same is true on the first day of fall, when the earth is on the opposite side of the sun.

If you keep watching, you'll see that about three months after the first day of spring, the top half of the earth now tilts toward the sun. The sun appears higher in the sky and is up for a longer period of time than in the other seasons. The sun's high position and longer days mean more heat to the top half of the earth. That's what gives us cozy—sometimes scorching—summer seasons.

Every winter we look forward to the warm relief and newness of spring. We know the joys of summer come next, followed by calm, quiet days of fall. Even in the midst of change, the rhythm of the seasons stays the same. Knowing that we can expect one season to follow another gives us something we can count on. It makes us feel secure.

While on this earth, there will always be lots of changes in our lives. But like the rhythm of the seasons, God always stays the same. He never changes. He's **immutable**. Knowing that God won't ever change gives us peace because it means we can count on Him. He makes us feel safe and secure.

How God treats us doesn't depend on how He happens to feel at the moment. He's not at all like humans in that way. He's never grouchy or moody, or too busy to listen. There are never times when He wants to be left alone, or when He's too sick to be bothered. God will never abandon us, and He can't die. His love, kindness, mercy, goodness, faithfulness—all His ways—are completely, perfectly constant. They never change.

Changes may come from surprising situations in our lives. They may come from the unexpected things other people do. We change, too. But as sure as spring follows winter and summer follows spring, we can count on God to stay the same.

In the northern hemisphere, the first day of winter—December 21 or 22—is the shortest day of the year.

equator: (ee-KWAY-ter) the imaginary line around the middle of the earth

In the northern hemisphere, the first day of summer—June 20, 21, or 22—is the longest day of the year.

immutable: (im-YOU-tuh-bul)

Thought to remember:

I can depend on God. He never changes.

Additional verses:

Numbers 23:19; Psalm 33:11; 102:25–27; Hebrews 13:8; James 1:17 (NIV)

Discover It!

Discover how the earth's tilt and movements around the sun cause seasons. You need a Styrofoam ball about the size of a tennis ball, a thin wooden dowel, and a lamp. Poke the dowel all the way through the middle of the ball. Remove the lampshade from the lamp and turn on the lamp. (Close any window shades or blinds if necessary.) Hold the ball about a foot away from the light bulb, tilting it so the rod is at a slight angle. *Keep the tilt the same* as you move the ball around the light. How do the tilt and orbit affect light on the Styrofoam "earth"?

Dig Deeper!

★ seasons

★ earth

★ sun

Is it really true that the sun rises every morning and sets at night? Before you answer, take a look at these simple facts about the earth and its movements around the sun.

As you probably already know, the earth is one of nine planets that circle the sun. The earth takes a little more than 365 days to complete one trip. While the earth makes that trip, it also spins, or **rotates**. Imagine a blue rubber ball. If you marked a black spot somewhere near the ball's middle and turned it, the spot would disappear from view. Now imagine the ball is the earth. The earth takes one whole day to rotate completely around. Twenty-four hours would pass before the dot returned to the place from which it started.

rotate: (ROW-tate)

Now that you know how the earth rotates as it circles the sun, is it really true that the sun rises every morning and sets at night?

From where you live on earth, it sure looks that way, doesn't it? But the answer is in the spin. As the earth circles the sun, it spins slowly from west to east. Because the earth spins toward the sun at sunrise, we think the sun is coming up in the east. As the earth continues to spin in the same direction, we move out of the sun's light at night, and the sun looks as if it's setting in the west.

> But LORD, you are a GOD who is tender and kind. You are gracious. You are slow to get angry. You are faithful and full of love.
>
> PSALM 86:15

Along with the earth's spin, there's another simple fact that affects sunrises and sunsets. Remember how the earth's slight tilt affects the seasons? The same tilt also affects lengths of days. During the summer when the northern hemisphere tilts toward the sun, the sun rises earlier and sets later. All the way at the top of the earth, at the north pole, the sun doesn't go down at all from about March 30 to September 23. During the winter, the opposite takes place—the sun rises later and sets earlier. At the north pole, the sun never comes up at all in winter!

When the sun stays up for twenty-four hours, it's called the midnight sun.

The fact that sunrises and length of days have to do with the earth's movements and tilt is fun to know about. But it doesn't really make that much difference in our lives, does it? What matters is that every morning the sun does come up, that it arcs across the sky, and then hides below the horizon again at night. What matters is that day after day, year after year, the sun is **faithful**. We depend on it!

faithful: loyal, steady in love and affection; can be counted on

If we look around the world, will we find anything as faithful as the sunrise? Probably not! Even the people who are important to us—the people we trust—let us down at one time or another. Our mothers, fathers, sisters, brothers, and best friends may love us, but sometimes they disappoint or hurt us.

If we can't count on those who are closest to us, then whom can we count on? The One who causes the earth to spin, tilt, and circle the sun today and every single day to come. God, who is faithful to keep the sun and earth on course, is just as faithful in our lives.

How is God faithful? He's loyal to us. He keeps His promises. He keeps us blameless. He strengthens and protects us. He doesn't let us get in over our heads when it comes to temptations. He protects us from the Evil One. He is always faithful to love us, too; no matter what, He always sticks with us.

In a world where even the most faithful person can let us down, God's faithfulness is refreshing. We can depend on Him because He's more faithful than a sunrise.

Thought to remember:

I can count on you, God. You are faithful.

Additional verses:

Psalm 33:4–5; 36:5; 136:2–9, 23; 145:13;
1 Corinthians 1:8–9; Galatians 5:22 (NIV);
1 Thessalonians 5:23–24

Perhaps you have a mother or father—or both—who aren't faithful to you. You wonder if you're even important to them because they often let you down by making promises and not keeping them. If your heart is hurting, climb into the Lord's lap. He'll dab your tears and wrap you in His arms. He is faithful. You can count on Him to be there for you.

Explore It!

See how the earth's movements affect sunrises and sunsets. Use the ball from "The Reasons for Seasons" on page 109. Mark the middle of the ball with a small dot.

Remove the lampshade from a lamp and turn on the lamp. Hold the ball in front of the lamp, with the dot facing the light. Slowly rotate the ball. As the ball spins, the dot moves out of the light. As the ball continues to turn, the dot moves back into the light. This is how the earth's movements bring sunrises and sunsets into our lives.

Now tilt the "earth" and move it around the "sun." How does the tilt affect sunrises and sunsets at the north and south poles?

DIG DEEPER!

* earth
* sun
* solar system
* geography

You're lost, hopelessly lost. There were two groups of hikers, one traveling at a quicker pace than the other. You decided to catch up to the faster group and thought you were on the right trail, but suddenly it ended. Disappeared. Instead of sitting tight and blowing the whistle your Dad gave you just in case something like this ever happened, you panicked and ran. Now there are trees everywhere, and they all look the same. And because each group thinks you're with the other, no one even knows you're missing. The urge to panic rises again. Stay calm. Breathe deeply. Think this through.

An idea surfaces through the confusion. Pray. *Help, Lord, I'm lost. You know exactly where I am. Pleeease show somebody where I am or give me directions to find the way out.* When you open your eyes, a sunny clearing is in view.

Ahh. The sun feels so good. The best thing to do is sit tight and wait. But while you're unwrapping a Snickers bar, another idea pops up. Before the hike this morning, your Dad checked the map. He pointed out how the trail begins at the river and runs along the east side of it for miles. You know you never crossed that river, so you must still be east of it. That means if you head west, you'll find the river—and the trail. You can stay here and wait, or you can head west. But how do you know which direction is west?

How would you find west if you were lost?

If you have a **compass**, finding west is easy. The needle inside the compass is magnetic. If you hold the compass in your hand, you will see that the north-seeking end of the needle points to magnetic north. Then you can twist the outside rim of the compass so that the "N"—which stands for north—lines up with the needle. After that you will be able to read markings on the compass to tell where south, east, and west are. If you're facing the same direction as the north-facing needle, south is the opposite direction. East is to the right of north, and west is to the left.

But what if you don't have a compass? If it's a sunny day, you can use the sun and

compass:
(KUM-pus)
an instrument used to tell directions

> **HE HAS REMOVED OUR LAWLESS ACTS FROM US AS FAR AS THE EAST IS FROM THE WEST.**
>
> PSALM 103:12

At NOON WHEN the SUN is overhead, your shadow will point NORTH.

Magnetic NORTH is about 1,500 miles away from the NORTH Pole, or true NORTH. To discover more about magnets, turn to "Irresistible Attraction" on page 42.

your shadow, though it's less accurate than a compass. We know the sun rises in the east and sets in the west. Before noon, your shadow will fall to the west of your body. If you face west, then you know east is behind you, north is on your right, and south is on your left. After noon, your shadow will fall to the east of your body. If you face east, then you know that west is behind you, north is on your left and south is on your right.

Figuring out where east and west are can bring relief when we're lost. Knowing east from west can also bring relief for another reason—when it comes to feeling guilty about sin.

God says that He has removed our sins as far as the east is from the west. How far is that?

Suppose you walked east. You kept walking through deserts and over mountains. At the ocean you got in a boat but continued to head east. Even if you walked clear around the world, you would still be going east. You would never meet west. East and west are as far as can be from each other!

So how far does God remove our sins from us? As far as can be. In other words, completely! In God's mind, once He forgives us of our sins, He forgets them. They are gone, vanished, vaporized. They have disappeared, and there is no trace.

Can you think of why it really matters whether our sins are completely removed? Here are some thoughts: Sin makes our hearts feel guilty. Then we can't come close to God, because we think there's something wrong between Him and us. The guilt is always there, like a wall that separates. Feeling guilty over sin is also a heavy burden to carry around in our hearts. It drags us down and can even make us sick.

But when we understand and believe that God has completely forgiven us, we feel relief. We have peace. It's a load off our hearts, and we can rest from carrying our burden of sin. Then we can come close to God.

It's important for us to believe that God completely forgives us. That's why knowing east from west brings us rest!

Have you ever done something wrong and asked to be forgiven, but the other person just can't seem to forget what you did? They bring it up every chance they get. God is not that way. He forgives us completely because of what Jesus has done for us. He gives us word pictures to make that clear. . . .

★ Have you ever spilled a red drink on white carpet? That stain is impossible to get out! Even though the stain of our sins is bright red, when we're forgiven, the stain becomes as white as snow (see Isaiah 1:18).

★ God says He puts all our sins behind His back, where He can't see them! (see Isaiah 38:17).

★ Our sins are swept away like clouds. They disappear like morning fog (see Isaiah 44:22).

★ God throws our sins into the bottom of the sea (see Micah 7:18–19).

Find It!

See if you can find north, south, east, and west.

★ If you have a compass, hold it flat and steady in your hand. The north-seeking needle will point to magnetic north, and the opposite end will point south. Which way are east and west?

★ Go outside on a sunny day. In the morning your shadow will fall to the west. At noon, it will point north. In the afternoon, it will fall to the east. Once you've located west, north, or east, find the other three directions.

DIG DEEPER!

★ magnets
★ compass
★ maps
★ geography

Thought to remember:

God forgives my sins and removes them as far as the east is from the west!

Additional verses:

Psalm 103:8–14; Isaiah 1:18; 38:17b; 44:22; Romans 8:1 (NIV); Hebrews 4:15–16; 10:22; 1 John 1:9

It's About Time

Have you ever noticed how our lives are wrapped around

time? Time is so important that our language is filled with expressions about it. Let's take a look at a few, one at a time. . . .

★ If you're pressed for time, you probably don't have time to breathe. You might find yourself wishing from time to time that you had time on your hands.

★ If you're having a good time, you're having the time of your life. Time flies when you're having fun, you know. But maybe at this point in time you're having a hard time. Seems like every time you turn around, someone is giving you a hard time.

Time is a big part of our lives, isn't it! We schedule our days based on the clock—when we have to be at school, when it's time to eat, get up, or go to bed. We mark the passing of time when we celebrate birthdays. Time always moves forward, and our lives move forward with it.

To discover more about how the earth spins and circles the sun, turn to "More Faithful Than a Sunrise" on page 112.

Because time is so important, we need ways to keep track of it. In the past, many civilizations kept track with the changes in the moon. Then the Egyptians began to follow the path of the sun across the sky. Today we still do the same thing; when the sun appears highest in the sky, we know we've reached twelve o'clock noon.

> HOLY, HOLY, HOLY IS THE LORD GOD ALMIGHTY, WHO WAS, AND IS, AND IS TO COME.
>
> REVELATION 4:8 (NIV)

There's a slight problem with basing daily times on when the sun is highest in the sky, though. The sun reaches its highest point in the sky at different times, depending on where you are. Large countries have many different noon times. To make life less confusing, people have divided the whole earth into twenty-four time zones, one for each hour of the day. Noon is set as the time when the sun reaches its highest point over the middle of each zone.

Greenwich: (GREH-nitch)

The zones start in **Greenwich**, near London, England. If you travel west from there, each time you pass into a new time zone your clock is turned back an hour. The opposite is true if you travel east. So if it's ten o'clock Saturday night in Greenwich, what time would it be in the time zone just west of it? Nine o'clock. And one zone to the east? Eleven o'clock.

Since God is eternal, He has no past, present, or future. We're different, though. Here on earth our lives are wrapped around time. The past is anything that happened just a second ago. The future is any moment that hasn't happened yet. The present is right now.

Sometimes people get caught in the trap of thinking about the past all the time, or worrying about the future. Doing that robs us of today. We can't fix the past, and we can't change the future. All we really have is the present, so it's best to live in the moment we have right now.

Find It!

Get out your atlas. If you don't have one, check the Internet or your library. In the index, look up "International Time Zones." This map will help you locate your time zone; Greenwich, England; and the International Date Line. Can you figure out why the International Date Line isn't straight?

The answer is on page 150.

Dig Deeper!

* time
* time zones
* calendar

Now suppose you traveled twelve zones to the west, all the way to the other side of the world. What time would it be? Ten o'clock Saturday morning. But if you traveled twelve zones to the east, it would be ten o'clock *Sunday* morning! On the other side of the world, where east and west time zones meet, there's a sudden jump from one day to the next. To divide one day from the next, an imaginary line—the International Date Line—runs north and south through the Pacific Ocean. On the east side of the International Date Line, you'll be a whole day ahead of someone on the west side of the line!

Since our lives are wrapped around time, it's hard to imagine what life would be like without it. Think of yourself as sailing through life in a time capsule. If you could jump out of the capsule—to be outside of time—what would your life be like?

There would be no nights or days—or seasons. You would have no birthdays, because you wouldn't grow older. You would always stay the same.

Imagining life without time helps us understand God a little better. Even though God made days and nights and seasons, they don't affect Him. He's outside the time capsule. He has no beginning or end. He doesn't change or grow old or die. Nobody made God—He always has been and always will be. He's **eternal**.

Trying to understand God's "beginningless" and endless life can give us brain meltdown. It's impossible to understand. He's amazing, isn't He! And do you know what else is amazing? At the moment we believe in Jesus, He gives *us* His eternal life. When our bodies wear out, our spirits continue to live on and on with God in heaven, where there is no time.

Our lives here on earth are centered around time. But our time here on earth can also be the beginning of life forever as we put our trust in Jesus.

Thought to remember:
God has no beginning or end. He is eternal.

Additional verses:
Job 36:26; Psalm 90:2 (NIV); 102:25–27; John 3:16; 1 Timothy 1:17 (NIV); 2 Peter 3:8

eternal:
(ee-TER-nul)
without beginning or end

gravity:
(GRAV-ih-tee)

Believe it or not, there's a strange attraction

going on between you and this book, the chair you're sitting in, the trees in your backyard, the moon, and the sun. There's even an attraction between you and the stars in the farthest reaches of the universe. It's always there, but most of the time you're probably not aware of it. What is it? **Gravity**.

What do we know about this strange force of attraction? A lot of our understanding began with a man who lived several centuries ago.

You've probably heard the adventures of Sir Isaac Newton and the apple tree. As this popular story goes, Newton was sitting under a tree when an apple fell and bonked him on the head. According to legend, it was this surprise encounter with an apple that led Newton to discover gravity.

Perhaps a falling apple really did hit Newton. But the truth is, people knew about gravity long before he did. This experience helped Newton realize that the force pulling the apple to earth is the same force pulling the moon into orbit around the earth. He saw that the force of gravity is active throughout the universe, drawing everything together.

Of course, the strength of the attraction between the earth and sun is much greater than between the earth and a faraway star. Why? The earth is much closer to the sun than a distant star. The strength of gravity's pull between two objects becomes less as the distance between them goes up. We can be thankful for that. If everything were drawn together with the same amount of force, the whole universe would be pulled into one jumbled mess!

An object's mass is always the same, but its weight can change depending on where it's measured

If there's a greater tug between objects that are close together, then why don't we feel the pull of gravity toward a book or another person? The strength of gravity's pull also depends on how much "stuff" an object is made of—its mass. We don't have a lot of mass, and neither does a book, so we don't feel the attraction that exists between us. But compared to us, the earth has a lot of mass. That's why we feel the power of gravity when we fall down!

> You believe there is one God. Good!
>
> JAMES 2:19a
>
> May the grace shown by the Lord Jesus Christ, and the love that God has given us, and the sharing of life brought about by the Holy Spirit be with you all.
>
> 2 CORINTHIANS 13:14

Because of gravity

* we have the directions *up* and *down*;

* the earth's atmosphere stays put;

* our planet is round;

* rain falls from the skies;

* the oceans' tides change twice a day;

* we enjoy sports such as skiing and skydiving.

Can you think of other ways this mysterious force shapes our lives?

Figure It!

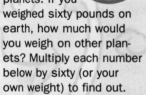

Figure out how much you would weigh on other planets. If you weighed sixty pounds on earth, how much would you weigh on other planets? Multiply each number below by sixty (or your own weight) to find out.

Mercury: .38 X 60 =

Venus: .90 X 60 =

Mars: .38 X 60 =

Jupiter: 2.54 X 60 =

Saturn: 1.07 X 60 =

Uranus: .92 X 60 =

Neptune: 1.19 X 60 =

Pluto: .06 X 60 =

The answers are on page 152.

What else do we know about gravity? It gives us weight. When we step on a scale, it measures just how much the earth's gravity pulls on us. Suppose you weigh sixty-five pounds on the earth. If you flew to the moon and stepped on a scale, would you weigh more or less? Since the moon has less mass than the earth, the force of gravity on the moon has less pull than on the earth. You would weigh less on the moon.

We have a good grasp on the different qualities of gravity. But even though we can explain a lot about it, there's one thing we don't know—what it is. Gravity is an unsolved mystery. Because humans are thirsty to explain the world around them, scientists today still search for answers about this mysterious force.

There are many unsolved mysteries in our lives. Another one has to do with who God is. In the Bible God makes it clear that there is only one God. Yet in the Old Testament when God speaks about himself, He sometimes uses a word that means "we" or "us." In the New Testament we discover that "we" means God the Father; Jesus Christ, the Son; and the Spirit of God. All have the same characteristics, or attributes, that only God has. How can one God be three distinct "persons"?

That is the mystery.

The fact that God is three persons in one stretches our limited minds. It's beyond understanding. But that's okay. This unsolved mystery shows us how awesome and great our God is compared to us.

Just as gravity is at work in our lives whether we know everything about it or not, so is God. He's at work drawing us to himself. Knowing God is much more important than understanding everything about Him. God the Father sent Jesus, the Son, so that we could know Him (see Matthew 11:27). He brings us into His family through His Spirit (see John 3:6).

We may never understand how God can be three persons in one. Even if we can't understand something about God, we can still believe it's true. And we can take joy in knowing the God who is beyond understanding.

Thought to remember:

Some things about God are mysteries, but I can get to know Him.

Additional verses:

Genesis 1:26a; Matthew 18:19; Mark 12:29;
2 Corinthians 3:17; 2 Thessalonians 1:2; 1 John 5:20

DIG DEEPER!

* gravity
* mass
* weight
* solar system

50 We All Fall Around

Did you know you're moving at nearly 67,000 miles per hour? "Impossible," you answer. "I'm sitting right here reading this; I'm not moving at all!"

But you are. We all are. The earth breezes around the sun at a breathtaking 67,000 miles per hour, and since we live on the earth, we **orbit** the sun with it. Wow! Who would guess we're tearing around the sun at such a fast clip?

It's a good thing we are.

You probably remember that gravity is the force that attracts objects to one another. It's the force that draws us to the sun and causes the earth to orbit around it.

Since gravity pulls the earth toward the sun, what keeps us from falling into it? The earth's speed—67,000 miles per hour—is what saves us from crashing into this hot ball of gases.

From experience you know that when you drop a ball, it falls straight to the ground. If you throw the ball away from you, it follows a curved path to the ground. Now imagine that you could throw a ball so hard that it soared really, really fast. What would happen to it? Without gravity, the ball would sail away in a straight line, off into the star-studded universe. Because of gravity, though, the ball is attracted to the earth while at the same time the speed of its forward motion keeps it from falling into the earth.

The earth is like the ball. Together, the balance of gravity and forward speed gives the earth a curved path—an orbit—around the sun. Another way to say this is that the earth falls *around* the sun.

The earth's curved path around the sun is not a circle. It's actually an **ellipse**, or oval shape. Here's why: Because the earth is going so fast, it blasts beyond the path of a circle to continue traveling away from the sun. Moving against the grip of gravity now, the earth loses speed and eventually stops moving away from the sun. The point where the earth stops moving away from the sun is also the point in the earth's

orbit: (OR-bit) the curved path that one heavenly body makes as it travels around another

To discover more about gravity, turn to "Unsolved Mysteries" on page 119 and "Four Forces" on page 140.

ellipse: (ee-LIPS)

> Let us keep looking to Jesus.
>
> HEBREWS 12:2a
>
> God is the God who gives peace. May He make you holy through and through. May your whole spirit, soul and body be kept free from blame. . . . The One who has chosen you is faithful. He will do all these things.
>
> 1 THESSALONIANS 5:23–24

apogee:
(AP-uh-jee)

perigee
(PEAR-ih-jee)

orbit where it's farthest from the sun. It's called the **apogee**. The point of the earth's orbit where it's closest to the sun is the **perigee**.

Gravity and speed are the reason the earth orbits the sun and doesn't fall into it. This same principle keeps planets, moons, and asteroids traveling around and around within our solar system. It's the reason the sun and a multitude of other stars stay in orbit as they wheel around the center of the Milky Way. There's a whole symphony of heavenly bodies that circle one another in the universe!

critical:
(KRIH-tih-kul)
very, very
important

There's no question about it. The fact that the earth orbits the sun is **critical** to our lives! And during our time on this planet, it's also critical that our lives orbit God, the Son. Orbit God, the Son? What does that mean?

It means that our attention and love are focused on Jesus, that He's the greatest treasure of our hearts. Focusing on God is important, because He desires our affection. He wants to be the center of our lives. God knows that if we orbit around Him, we will truly be satisfied in life.

There are lots of things in this world to distract us from God as we move forward in our lives. Sometimes our focus turns to people we want to get affection and approval from. Sometimes our focus turns to things that bring instant pleasure. Sometimes our focus even turns to our problems. Even if we lose our focus, though, the Lord is faithful. God, the One who conducts the symphony of the universe, also keeps us in "orbit" around himself. He's always faithful to keep us in orbit around the Son!

Thought to remember:
My life orbits around Jesus.

Additional verses:
Psalm 27:4; Matthew 6:21 (NIV); Philippians 1:6; 4:8; Hebrews 12:1–2a; 1 John 5:4–5

Scientists discovered the planet Neptune by watching the orbit of Uranus. They figured that "wobbles" in Uranus's orbit were caused by the gravitational pull of a nearby, unknown planet. This resulted in a search that led to the discovery of Neptune. The wobbles in Uranus's and Neptune's orbits also caused scientists to search for another planet. That's how Pluto was discovered, though it's now known that Pluto is too small to cause the wobbling. Could there be a tenth planet?

Make It!

Make an orbit like the earth's! All you need is an eight-inch square of thick cardboard, two plastic thumbtacks, a ten-inch piece of string tied in a loop, and a pencil. Poke the tacks near the middle of the cardboard, about three inches apart. Label one of the tacks the "sun." Place the loop of string over the thumbtacks. Stick the pencil inside the loop and pull the string snug against the thumbtacks. Using the string as a guide, draw an ellipse with your pencil. Notice how one end of the orbit is farther from the sun than the other.

DIG DEEPER!
* orbit
* solar system
* earth, sun
* satellites

You could float on a boat in the Greenland Sea or ride the rails through Italy. You could fly a balloon over Timbuktu or trek on a mountain that's called K-2. But no matter where you are, and no matter what you do, the same face of the moon always shines down on you.

The moon is a familiar form in our skies. It's large and close to our world, so we can often spot the moon during the day, as well as at night. As it journeys around the earth, we circle the sun together. Both earth and moon are about the same distance from the sun. But that doesn't mean the moon is like our planet. To understand what the moon is like, all you have to remember is the word *no*. Our pale partner has no air, no wind, no water, no weather, and no life. There are reasons for that.

The moon is our nearest neighbor. It's nearly 239,000 miles away—a three-day trip by spacecraft.

There may not be life on the moon, but man has visited the moon six times. The first landing was on July 20, 1969.

Our constant companion is only about one-fourth the size of the earth and has less mass. Do you remember how the strength of gravity's pull goes up with an increase in the mass of an object? Less mass means less gravity. And less gravity means the moon couldn't hold on to a blanket of air even if there ever was one. Without an atmosphere, there can be no wind, weather, water—or life. That's why you won't find mice or men or monkeys on the moon.

Because the moon is such a close neighbor, humans have always followed its movements. We hear about it in songs, stories, and sayings. Our words for *Monday* and *month* come from an old English word for moon. Calendars have even been based on the rhythms of its monthly trip around the earth. These calendars were based on the moon's shape.

We all display the Lord's glory. We are being changed to become more like Him so that we have more and more glory. And the glory comes from the Lord, who is the Holy Spirit.

2 CORINTHIANS
3:18b

Phase: (FAZE)

You've probably noticed how the moon's face seems to change from night to night; the changing faces of the moon are called **phases**. As it travels around the earth, we see different amounts of the moon's face lit by sunlight. What does sunlight have to do with moonlight? Moonlight *is* sunlight that bounces, or reflects, off the moon's surface.

The phases begin when the moon is between the earth and sun. In this first phase only the far side of the moon is lit by sunshine and we can't see it. As the moon moves

crescent:
(KRESS-ent)

east, it appears to grow slowly, or wax. We now see a sliver of light that looks like a friendly sideways smile, or **crescent** moon. Each day, the light grows until we see a half-moon. When the earth is between the sun and moon, the face of our nearest neighbor appears round and full, like a giant pearl.

Then the moon orbits around the other side of the earth and appears to shrink, or wane. Soon the moon decreases to half size again. With each day, the silvery light retreats until we see only that skinny sideways smile again. When the moon reaches the spot where it started, one journey around the earth is complete.

Sometimes during different phases the moon looks milky. Sometimes it's silvery bright, sometimes golden or red. No matter which phase or what color, the moon's shining beauty comes from the reflected light of the sun.

In a way, you could say we are like the moon. When we make the choice to become followers of Jesus, we become reflectors of His light. The moon couldn't produce light even if it tried. We can't produce light, either. If the world sees God's beauty in us, it's because we reflect His light.

While He was here on earth, Jesus made it clear that He spoke only the words that His Father gave Him to speak. The same is true of the Holy Spirit when He speaks to us. His job is to speak only what He hears. And we're no different. God desires for us to say what He tells us to say and do what He prepares us to do.

The trouble is, many of us want to shine for God so much that sometimes we try to do the work ourselves—we try to make our own light. We may think that if we just try harder, we'll see God do more work in the lives of our friends who need His healing touch. A lot of times we impatiently rush ahead, instead of waiting for Jesus to lead.

The moon doesn't worry about shining. It hangs where God put it, turning and revolving and reflecting the sun's light. We don't have to worry about shining, either. Wherever we are, we can trust God's Son to shine on us for all the world to see!

These are the basic phases of the moon:

new moon
↓
crescent moon (waxing)
↓
half-moon (waxing)
↓
full moon
↓
half-moon (waning)
↓
crescent moon (waning)

Here are more marvelous moon facts:

* The pull of the moon's gravity causes the rise and fall of ocean tides on earth.

* The surface of the moon consists mainly of craters, highlands, and wide plains.

* Because there's no wind or rain on the moon, the footprints of astronauts could remain forever.

* To tell whether the moon is waxing or waning, make a circle around the moon with both hands. If the moon is waxing, the shiny rounded part will be on the right side. If it's waning, the shiny rounded part will be on the left side.

CHECK IT Out!

To check out the reflection of light, all you need is a piece of aluminum foil, a flashlight, and a dark room.

Hold the foil in front of your face inside the dark room. Can you see it? Now turn on the flashlight and point it toward the foil. Notice how the foil reflects light—like the moon!

The same side of the moon always faces us. That's because the moon spins around only once as it circles the earth once. To see for yourself, all you need is a glass and a small ball.

Place a dot on the ball with a marker. Pretend this is the moon. Place the glass in front of you; pretend it's the earth. Now face the dot on the "moon" toward the "earth." Slowly move the "moon" around the "earth," making sure the dot always faces the glass. As the moon circles the earth once, it will also spin completely around one time, keeping its near side toward us.

DIG DEEPER!

* moon
* earth
* solar system

Thought to remember:

I'm a reflector of God's light.

Additional verses:

John 6:28–29; 8:28b; 13:16; 14:10, 24; 16:13; 2 Corinthians 3:18; 4:6

52 Sun Life

Suppose you took a giant leap into space, beyond our galaxy, the Milky Way. Looking back, what would you see?

You'd see a lot of stars, all right—so many stars that the Milky Way appears hazy. But could you find the sun? It's not very likely. Our sun may be a big blinding spot in the sky when viewed from the earth, but compared to other stars it's just plain—well, ordinary. Ho-hum. Average. Our very own star, the sun, is medium sized, of medium temperature, and of medium brightness.

The sun isn't the biggest and brightest, but that's a good thing. Why? Because if it were any bigger or brighter, the earth would be scorched—and so would we. And if it were smaller or dimmer, we would freeze. Our very own star is positively the perfect size and brightness to bring life to the earth—and that makes it outshine all the other stars in the universe.

Can you think of ways the sun supports life on earth?

Because of the sun . . .

The earth receives the gift of warmth. Without it, our earth would be nothing more than a **desolate** rock. Like light, heat forms at the very heart—or core—of the sun, taking years to rise through thick layers to the surface, or **photosphere**. And even though the earth absorbs only a very tiny amount of the total energy the sun sends out, it's just the right amount. That energy influences our seasons. It's responsible for the variety of plant and animal life that covers our planet.

> **FOR to me, to Live is CHRIST.**
>
> PHILIPPIANS 1:21a (NIV)

Because of the sun . . .

The earth receives the gift of light. Plants can grow. They turn sunlight into energy for themselves, the animals that eat them, and other animals that eat the animals that eat plants. Since sunshine is where all food begins, you could say that whether you eat plants or meat, you're eating sunshine! As strange as it may sound, you could also say that when you breathe, you're breathing sunshine, too. How? Plants give off oxygen as they turn sunshine into food. We depend on plants—and the sun—to renew the air we breathe.

Because of the sun . . .

We enjoy clouds that float by and the rain they bring. Heat from the sun causes water

---

How big is the sun? It's 865,000 miles across—big enough to fit one million earths inside!

desolate: (DES-uh-Let) Lifeless; dreary and deserted

photosphere: (FO-toe-sfear) the brightest layer of the sun we see from earth!

To discover more about how the sun produces energy, turn to "Shine!" on page 134.

To discover more about clouds and wind turn to "A Cat, a King, an Angel's Wing" on page 73, and "A Whisper of Wind" on page 71.

Ready for more fun sun facts?

* It takes about eight minutes for heat, light, and other forms of energy to travel 93 million miles from the sun to the earth.

* The outermost layer of the sun's atmosphere is the **corona** (kuh-ROW-nuh). Some of the sun's electrically charged particles escape through the corona to become the solar wind.

* The northern and southern lights are shimmering displays of lights that also have their beginnings in solar wind.

* Sometimes extra energy bursts from the surface of the sun. These solar flares can interrupt radio signals, shut down electrical power, and increase displays of northern lights.

Explore It!

Unscramble these words to reveal ways that the sun affects the earth.

i g l t h

o d o f

d w n i

u s l d c o

r i a

e f l u

t t e e i i y l c c r

m t r a w h

f i l e

The answers are on page 151.

Dig Deeper!

* sun
* earth
* solar system
* stars

to evaporate and form clouds. It warms the air to create winds. And if that's not enough, the sun plays a huge role in providing us with fuels to give us the convenience of electricity, run our cars, and heat our homes. We can thank our local star for coal, oil, natural gas, windmills, waterpower, and solar cells, because they all have their beginnings in the sun.

Wow! Our sun is much more than a bright spot in our skies! The sun gives life to our planet.

Two thousand years ago, a man named Jesus walked on this earth. Like the sun, there wasn't anything outwardly special about Jesus. He wasn't handsome enough to attract people or make them notice Him (Isaiah 53:2).

Like the sun, Jesus is also a giver of life. He's *the* giver of life. Even though Jesus was the Son of God and had never sinned, He took responsibility for our sins. He died on a cross, giving up His own life. Jesus died, was buried, and rose from the grave, never to die again. Believing that Jesus took responsibility for our sins makes us right with God. What difference does that make?

Because of Jesus . . .

We have new life in our spirits. Before we believe in Jesus, our spirits are like the earth without the warmth of the sun—frozen and desolate. But Jesus breathes new life into our spirits. He gives us eternal life, life with Him that lasts forever.

Because of Jesus . . .

We can grow. Day by day, God's Spirit feeds and leads and teaches us. He is food for our hearts.

Because of Jesus . . .

We have new meaning for our lives. In Jesus we have a new purpose and reason for waking up every morning! We can have lives that are full and satisfying. Life becomes more than a dead-end street.

There's a lot to the life we have in Jesus. Explore how He brings life to you!

Thought to remember:
Jesus is my life.

Additional verses:
John 10:10b; 14:6; Romans 6:23; 2 Corinthians 5:21; Ephesians 2:8; Colossians 3:2–4; 1 John 5:11

On many nights of the year, the far northern and southern skies of the world transform into a stage—a stage for dancing lights. Perhaps you've seen them. . . .

The ballet begins with a soft green glow that spreads across the dark sky. Leaping into a graceful arc, the green deepens. It twists and twirls, bends and curls, as if pulsing to the sounds of a silent symphony. With a burst, the arc explodes with color. A red veil ripples across the stage. Pink, green, and white rays streak the night sky. Then the dance slows. Just as they appeared, the lights fade from the stage and disappear into the night.

What causes these spectacular colors to dance across the night sky stage?

Three ingredients are needed to produce northern lights, or **aurora borealis**, as they're called in the northern hemisphere.

The first ingredient is solar wind. It's made of electrically charged particles that escape from the sun's atmosphere and stream out into space.

Since solar wind travels in every direction at high speeds, some reaches the earth. That brings up a second ingredient that plays a role in forming northern lights: the earth's magnetic field. Called the **magnetosphere**, the earth's magnetic field acts like a giant shield to protect us from the sun's charged particles. As the solar wind hits the magnetosphere, most of the particles are forced to flow around the earth. But some of the charged particles pass through the earth's protective magnetic shield, drawn toward the earth's north and south poles. And that's where the third ingredient for the northern lights comes in—gases in the earth's atmosphere.

As charged particles invade the earth's magnetosphere, they reach the earth's atmosphere, which is made up mostly of nitrogen and oxygen gases. When charged particles crash into atoms and molecules of these gases, the atoms become "excited." They give off different colors of light—pinkish reds, blues and purples, greens and whites. The color depends on which gas the particles hit, as well as how high they are in the atmosphere.

There's no question about it. A performance of dancing lights is such a showstopper it can make you want to dance inside! These shimmering colors are so startling

aurora borealis: (uh-ROAR-uh boar-ee-AL-us) means "northern dawn"

South of the equator, dancing lights are called southern lights, or aurora australis (aw-STRAY-lus). It means "southern dawn."

magnetosphere: (mag-NEE-toe-sfear)

To discover more about the atmosphere, turn to "Inside, Outside, All Around" on page 69.

To discover more about light, turn to "Shining Light on Light" on page 18.

> This is the day the Lord has made; let us rejoice and be glad in it.
>
> PSALM 118:24
> (NIV)

The largest number of auroras takes place every eleven years. That's because every eleven years or so, the number of sunspots—dark patches on the sun's surface—increases. This causes a rise in the number of solar flares exploding from the sun's surface, which also causes more charged particles to be released into space. More charged particles means that more atoms in the earth's atmosphere will be struck to create more dancing lights. This also means people living farther away from the north and south poles will be treated to fantastic displays of light. These solar storms can also cause radio transmission and electrical problems on earth. The last increase in solar flares took place in the year 2000. When will the next one probably take place?

List It!

Grab a pen and paper and find an out-of-the-way place. Sit quietly; think about God and all the special things He does for you. Ask Him to show you the many ways He is in your life. List these blessings as God reveals them to you. Tell God how much you appreciate Him and all He does.

Discover It!

Take a discovery walk around the block, through a park, or in your backyard. Take time to stop, look, listen, smell, and feel snow, rocks, flowers, the sky—anything around you. What details are new to you? Whenever you're out and about, make a habit of stopping to notice the world around you. Beauty is everywhere.

DIG DEEPER!

* northern, southern lights
* aurora borealis, australis
* solar wind

that their beauty still surprises those who have seen them many times.

In our spiritual lives we also have dancing-light days. These are times when God's presence is so real we feel as if we could reach out and touch Him. They're times when we see spectacular miracles or amazing answers to prayer. Dancing-light times in our spiritual lives are exciting and encouraging.

But dancing lights don't show up every day of the year. And the same is true in our spiritual lives, too. What do we do on plain old ordinary days?

We look for everyday wonders to rejoice in: moon sparkles on a lake . . . leaves clapping in a breeze . . . floating dandelion seeds lit from behind by the sun.

In a similar way, we can rejoice in God for many simple blessings. We can rejoice in the quiet comfort we receive by going to our Father with a hurt . . . seeing God's love for us through a friend . . . thinking about His beauty and greatness.

No one will argue that dancing lights and miracles are great to experience. But it's important to remember that there are less spectacular events that can also bring us joy. They happen every day. If we look for them, our lives will be rich.

Thought to remember:

I can rejoice in simple blessings. They'll make my life rich!

Additional verses:

Psalm 4:7; 27:4; 37:4a; 118:1; Romans 11:33–36 (NIV); Philippians 4:8; 1 John 3:1

The year is 3001. Earth is overcrowded. You've been chosen to help build a colony on another planet. Before you are eight curtains. Behind each curtain is a planet from our solar system. As they open, you'll get a virtual experience of what each planet is like. Pay attention, because after you've "visited" each one, you'll cast a vote. Which world will you decide to live on?

The first curtain opens and Mercury appears. Closest to the sun, it's the first and smallest of four "rocky planets." One day on Mercury takes fifty-nine Earth days! Daytime temperatures soar to eight hundred degrees Fahrenheit, nighttime temperatures sink to minus three hundred degrees. Watch out—a meteor! There's no atmosphere to burn up meteors on Mercury. That's why so many craters dot the otherwise boring, smooth surface. Kind of reminds you of the moon. Speaking of moons, there aren't any.

Mercury could take some getting used to. Let's check Venus.

Earth's twin? It may be similar in size and mass, but that's about all. This planet rotates so slowly, one day takes 243 Earth days! A crushing atmosphere, choking clouds of **sulfuric** acid, and nine-hundred-degree temperatures also leave a lot to be desired. It's pretty neat that Venus rotates backward, though, and volcanic mountains perk up the plains. Let's continue.

Mars is fourth from the sun. Hmm. Interesting rusty color. Mars tilts like Earth, so it has seasons, but they're almost twice as long as ours. Those channels, volcanoes, and deep canyons are interesting. So are the two oddly shaped moons. Strong winds, freezing temperatures, and a thin atmosphere would make this planet hard to live on, too.

Now we move on to the giant gas planets. Raise curtain four! We would get dizzy on Jupiter, the largest of all planets. It completes one day in less than ten hours. Its colorful bands, Great Red Spot, faint ring, and sixteen moons make it a pretty peculiar planet. This planet radiates more heat than it receives from the sun. But wait, there's a problem here. We can't land on a surface that's mostly hydrogen, a gas!

The rocky planets are Mercury, Venus, Earth, and Mars. They're made mostly of rock and iron.

Sulfuric: (Sul-FYUR-ik) containing sulfur. Clouds of sulfuric acid would be very poisonous!

The giant gas planets are Jupiter, Saturn, Uranus, and Neptune. They're made mostly of gases.

So we fix our eyes not on what is seen, but on what is unseen. For what is seen is temporary, but what is unseen is eternal.

2 CORINTHIANS 4:18 (NIV)

What is the heavenly world like? The heavenly world we belong to is much more beautiful than anything here on Earth. Heaven is a city made of gold and jewels. It's a place where there won't be any tears, pain, or death. This special city doesn't need the light of the sun or moon because God is there and His glory is so bright. And that's what's best about heaven. In heaven we'll see our Jesus face-to-face! You can read about heaven in Revelation, chapter 21.

Here's a sentence to help you remember the order of all nine planets. The first letter of each word is the same as the first letter of a planet. **M**y **V**ery **E**ager **M**other **J**ust **S**erved **U**s **N**ine **P**ies (Mercury, Venus, Earth, Mars, Jupiter, Saturn, Uranus, Neptune, Pluto).

Let's open curtain five. Saturn. Here's a planet that may be second in size, but not in beauty. Saturn's seven rings and yellowish surface make it a planet of distinction. This ringed planet is so light it could float on water. Its eighteen moons are captivating. Slight problem here, too. Saturn's surface is also made of gases.

On to Uranus. We're getting way out here, now. A bluish green atmosphere made of hydrogen, helium, and a poisonous gas covers this seventh planet. Strange, but Uranus's thin, dark rings tilt up and down, not sideways! Uranus would have unbearably long seasons because of its funny tilt and long years.

Better try Neptune, the deep blue planet. A quick look tells us Neptune is similar to Uranus. Neptune has eight moons, long years, a poisonous atmosphere, and a Great Dark Spot similar to Jupiter's. . . .

Let's lift the eighth and final curtain. Pluto. Brr. This tiniest of planets is icy, with surface temperatures nearly four hundred degrees below zero. One day on Pluto takes about six Earth days. One year is equal to about 250 of our own. Not a fun place to live!

Which world would you choose? That's an impossible choice! None of these planets come close to fitting our needs for life. Knowing about the other planets makes us feel snug on our third planet from the sun. But we don't want to get too snug—

God gave us Earth, the perfect planet to live on and take care of. But if we belong to Him, this world isn't really our true home, either. We're strangers here. We're citizens of another world that lasts forever—heaven. It's a spiritual world that, for now, we see with our hearts, not with our eyes.

Once we become citizens of heaven, God wants us to live for Him—He becomes our **priority**. God wants our affection; He wants us to depend on Him. While we live here on Earth, we can be tempted to have a different attitude, though. We can be tempted to live for ourselves and for the pleasures of sin . . . long to own things we don't have . . . boast about what we've done and how important we are.

Sometimes living for these things is easier than living for God and His world that we see only with our hearts. That's

Pluto isn't a rock or gas planet. Made of frozen gas and ice, it's in a class by itself. Some scientists even wonder if Pluto is truly a planet.

To discover more about Earth, turn to "Our Place in Space" on page 106.

priority: (pry-OR-ih-tee) the thing that's most important

132

why we need to remember that we belong to God, and why we make a choice every day: which world?

Thought to remember:

This world isn't my true home. I belong to God.

Additional verses:

1 Corinthians 6:19–20; Philippians 3:20; Hebrews 11:13–16; 1 Peter 1:17–19; 1 John 2:15–17

Match It!

Match each description below with the right planet.

largest planet	
lots of craters	
rust colored	
farthest from the sun (most of the time)	Mercury
shortest day	Venus
Great Dark Spot	
Great Red Spot	Mars
clouds of sulfuric acid	Jupiter
rings tilted up and down	
bluish green	Saturn
closest to the sun	
rotates backward	Uranus
seven large rings	Neptune
two small, oddly shaped moons	
deep blue	Pluto
smallest planet	
longest day	

The answers are on page 151.

DIG DEEPER!

★ solar system
★ planets
★ names of individual planets

133

Remember this rhyme?

Twinkle, twinkle, little star,
How I wonder what you are.
Up above the world so high
Like a diamond in the sky.
Twinkle, twinkle, little star,
How I wonder what you are.

You've probably heard this rhyme as many times as there are stars in the Milky Way. What are those lights that twinkle like a diamond in the sky? And what makes them shine?

A star is a super-hot ball of gases. At its heart is a fiery furnace made mostly of hydrogen, a gas. There's so much pressure at the center of a star that it creates extreme heat. Extreme heat and pressure can force together protons—the tiny particles at the center of hydrogen atoms. When this happens, it sets off a chain of reactions. The hydrogen protons are changed into particles of a different gas, helium, and huge amounts of energy are given off. Some of that energy is light—and that's what makes a star shine!

Most stars look like silver freckles when we peer at them from earth. But stars come in all kinds of sizes. Like jewels of the universe, they also come in all kinds of colors—reds, oranges, yellows, whites, and blues. The color of a star gives us an idea about its temperature. Red stars are the coolest; their surface temperatures are only about 5,000 degrees Fahrenheit. Orange stars are hotter, followed by yellow, white-yellow, white, blue-white, and blue. Temperatures on the surface of some blue stars sizzle at way over 50,000 degrees!

Size and color aren't the only qualities that are hard to distinguish with our eyes alone. The brightness of different stars is also hard to tell apart. You may have noticed that most stars look pretty much the same. But **astronomers**, scientists who

Well, maybe you haven't heard the rhyme quite that many times. It's believed there are over 100 BILLION stars in our galaxy!

Our Sun is a yellow star. Its surface is about 10,000 degrees.

astronomer: (uh-STRAW-nuh-mer)

> Among the people of the world you shine like stars in the heavens. You shine as you hold out to them the word of life.
>
> PHILIPPIANS
> 2:15b–16a

study stars, have discovered that some stars are much brighter than others. Just how dazzling a star is has a lot to do with its color. Cooler red stars are usually the dimmest. Can you guess which stars are the brightest? That's right, the hottest blue stars are also the most brilliant.

There are some exceptions, though. Supergiants are gigantic red stars with cool surface temperatures. Because they're so large, though, they give off huge amounts of light and are very bright. White dwarfs, on the other hand, are so tiny that even though they're white-hot, they give off only small amounts of light. As you might guess, they're dim.

A star shines brightly because energy flows from its fiery furnace to its surface. Can you think of another reason we can see stars? Contrast. The contrast of bright light against darkness makes it possible for us to enjoy these shining points of light. When the sky is pale—as it is during the day—there's no contrast between stars and the sky. Even though stars shine all day, they don't stand out against the sky and we can't see them!

Did you know that God also wants you to shine like the stars? When Jesus came into this world, He came as a light. Jesus' light was so bright, He was a great contrast to a world darkened by sin. He was like the brightest of blue stars shining out of a pitch-black night!

When Jesus returned to heaven, did light completely vanish from this world? No! Whoever believes in Jesus has His light in their heart. God continues to shine His light into this dark world through the people who believe in Him. If you believe in Jesus, you're a shining star, too.

Contrast is what makes you shine like a star. As you walk with Jesus, your life and behavior will stand out—it will be a contrast to those around you who don't know Jesus. Even if you don't say a word, others will notice God's bright life inside you. If they're searching for Jesus, they'll be drawn to Him as a bug is drawn to light!

Thought to remember:

As I walk with Jesus I will shine like a star!

Additional verses:

Matthew 5:14–16; John 1:4–5, 9; John 3:21;
2 Corinthians 4:6; 2 Corinthians 5:17–18

Scientists measure the brightness of stars two ways. The first one measures how dazzling a star looks from earth—no matter how far away it is. As you might guess, our sun shines brightest of all when measured this way.

The second method compares the brightness of stars as if they were all the same distance from the earth. This gives a better idea of how brilliant a star actually is.

CHECK It Out!

To check out how contrast makes a difference, all you need is a flashlight. On a sunny day go outside with your flashlight. Turn it on. How well can you see the light beam in daylight? Then, go outside on a moonless night and turn on your flashlight. Now how well can you see the light? The contrast is much greater when it's dark, isn't it!

DIG DEEPER!

* stars
* universe
* astronomy

Have you ever looked up at the stars and wondered

how big the universe really is? Fasten your seat belt and see for yourself. It's time for a spaceship trip through the universe. Full speed ahead!

The journey begins at our blue planet, about 93 million miles from our sun. As you travel away from the earth, you see that it is only one of nine known planets in our solar system. Pluto, the ninth planet, is about 4.6 billion miles away from the sun.

Those distances—93 *million* and 4.6 **billion**—miles might not seem like much, but have you ever thought about what a million is? If you counted to a million at the speed of one number per second, it would take you about eleven and a half days to reach a million. Counting to a billion would take you nearly thirty-two years. Traveling to Pluto is going to be a l-o-o-o-n-n-n-g, cold trip.

But that's nothing, because when you streak past Pluto, you discover that our sun is only one of over 100 billion stars in the Milky Way, the galaxy where we live. The Milky Way is so vast that out here distance is measured in light-years. A light-year is how far a ray of light travels in one year. Put in math terms, light travels at 186,000 miles per second. That means in one year, light travels nearly six **trillion** miles. The Milky Way is so huge that even if we switched from our spaceship to ride on a light beam, a trip from one side to the other would take us 100,000 years.

But that's nothing when you see that the Milky Way is only one of about 100 *billion galaxies*. Pictures taken by the Hubble Space Telescope show that the number may be even larger. Think about it. Billions of stars in one galaxy. Billions of galaxies in the universe. With all these stars, you'd think the universe would be pretty crowded and as bright as a light bulb. But it's as dark as the bottom of the ocean out there. The universe is so big and the stars are so far apart that

billion: 1,000 million

No one knows for sure how big the universe is. But many scientists believe the universe is still expanding. It's thought that all parts of the universe are spreading away from other parts.

trillion: a number way, way bigger than a billion. A trillion is 1,000 billion.

To discover more about this space telescope, turn to "Eyes on the Skies" on page 143.

> Lord, you have seen what is in my heart. You know all about me. You know when I sit down and when I get up. You know what I'm thinking even though you are far away. You know when I go out to work and when I come back home. You know exactly how I live. I'm amazed at how well you know me. It's more than I can understand.
>
> PSALM 139:1–3, 6

most of it is empty space.

But all that's still nothing when you realize God is greater than the universe. He put all these stars in place. He knows exactly how many stars there are. He knows each one's name.

Seeing how big the universe is and how the earth is barely a speck in space could make a person feel pretty small and unimportant. But it doesn't have to. God sees past every single one of those stars to the earth. He sees past the more than six billion people who live here—to you! Not only does God see you, but He knows you, too. And He loves you more than you could imagine. God's love for you is bigger than the universe.

There may be days when you don't feel very important. Maybe you had a bad day because of problems at school or home. If the night is clear, look up at the stars. Remember that God knows your name. He knows all about you. He loves you. You're His star.

WITH LOVE

He that shaped the heavens
Vast above your sight
Set the stars like diamonds
Against black velvet night.
Silvery, sparkling, flawless,
God's glory they proclaim.
Countless, yet God counts them all
And calls each one by name.
If when you see the stars at night,
Your life seems small and dim,
Consider what God says to you.
Listen now to Him.
The stars He made, yes, bright and full
And set them high above,
And like the stars He calls your name—
But whispers yours with love.

Thought to remember:

God knows my name. I'm His star.

Additional verses:

Job 9:8–10; Psalm 8:3–4; 147:4–5; Isaiah 43:1b, 4a; 49:16; Ephesians 3:18–19; 1 John 4:9–10

Billions of stars in billions of galaxies? No one knows how many stars there really are. Without a telescope about three thousand stars can be seen on a dark night. Different stars come into view throughout the year, so a total of six thousand can be observed without a telescope. Almost every star you see with the naked eye is part of our Milky Way Galaxy. The only other galaxy you can see with your eyes alone is the Andromeda Galaxy.

Using the most powerful telescopes, astronomers bring the number of stars up to 10 billion trillion. But that's only an **estimate** (ES-tih-mit: a good guess). Only God knows for sure how many stars there are. And He knows each one by name!

Discover It!

Still wondering how much a million is? Discover it for yourself. Start a collection and try to reach a million. Some ideas for collectibles are beads, popcorn, soda can tabs, or pennies. If you decide to collect a million pennies, figure out how many dollars that would make. (Hint: Divide one million by one hundred.) This is a good activity to share with your class or another group. You'll also find the book *How Much Is a Million?* by David M. Schwartz helpful

Find It!

Use a star chart to find the Andromeda Galaxy (also called M31). A star chart can be found at *www.skymaps.com*. Once you find it on the star map, find it in the night sky with a pair of binoculars. It will look like a fuzzy blob made up of many stars.

DIG DEEPER!

* astronomy
* universe
* galaxy
* stars

57 Secret of the Stars

Space travelers beware—there are invisible beasts lurking among the stars. Disguised by darkness, they lie in wait to swallow anything that strays too close. You never know they're out there until it's too late. . . .

Maybe the idea of black holes sounds like science fiction to you. But astronomers have strong evidence suggesting that black holes, the secret of the stars, really do exist. Even though we can't see them, let's take a look.

It's believed that black holes are dead stars. How can stars "die"? All stars, including our sun, behave like giant furnaces sending heat and light into space. But when a star runs out of fuel, it dies. When it no longer produces energy to push out against the pull of its own gravity, the star collapses. All the matter it's made of is crushed into a small, tightly packed ball. As a result, the gravitational force of this collapsed star now becomes as monstrously big as the star is small.

To discover more about gravity, turn to "Unsolved Mysteries" on page 119.

Stars the size of our sun shrink into white dwarfs when they die. Stars bigger than our sun are believed to become neutron stars. But the largest of stars may shrink into those invisible beasts of the universe, black holes. The gravitational pull of black holes is so great that not even light can escape. And that's what makes a black hole invisible.

> Love each other deeply. Honor others more than yourselves.
>
> ROMANS 12:10

Why can't light escape from a black hole? The reason has to do with something we're all familiar with here on earth: escape speed. When you throw a baseball into the air, what happens? The ball falls back to your hands; it's not going fast enough to escape the pull of the earth's gravity. But a rocket can escape the forces of the earth because it's supplied with enough power to break free of the earth's pull. Our sun, much larger than the earth, has a much greater gravitational pull. A whole lot more speed would be needed to break away from its gravity. But the gravitational pull of a black hole is monstrous compared to the gravitational pull of the sun. The gravitational pull of a black hole is so great not even light—which travels faster than anything else known—travels fast enough to escape it.

If black holes are invisible, then how could scientists possibly hunt them down? One clue came from watching other stars. Scientists noticed that some stars appear to orbit something that can't be seen. The unseen body the star is orbiting might just be a black hole. Why? A short distance from these stars, large amounts of X rays have been discovered. These X rays may come from the star's gases and other matter as they're pulled in by the black hole's powerful gravitational force.

Another clue provides further proof of black holes. In some areas of space, light bends for unknown reasons. Perhaps light bends as it passes by a black hole.

Scientists exploring farther into space are likely to discover more about black holes. Whether or not black holes are exactly as we now picture them, one thing is sure. Something with a strong gravitational force is swallowing matter and light in space.

As strange as it may sound, there are also black holes here on earth. Perhaps you know some. They're self-centered people who swallow up all the attention of others around them. When they talk, they focus only on themselves or their own interests. They seem uninterested in others around them. When it comes to activities, they only want to take part in the activities they're excited about. Black-hole people are so in to themselves, you get the feeling it doesn't even matter if you're there. Being around them is tiring. It sucks the life right out of you.

What can you do about a person who reminds you of a black hole? Not a whole lot. God didn't put us on earth to change others. But there is one thing each of us can do—be sure we're not black holes ourselves. How?

Develop an honest and sincere interest in others. Ask questions to find out about their lives. When they talk, listen carefully and you'll get to know them. Go out of your way to make them feel special. Serve them as Jesus served others while He was on earth.

Getting your eyes off of yourself and taking an interest in others helps develop strong friendships. Plus, you become a more fun and interesting person to be around!

Thought to remember:
Don't be a black hole. Develop an interest in others.

Additional verses:
Mark 10:43–45; Romans 14:7; 15:1–3a;
1 Corinthians 13:4–5; 1 John 4:9–11

Many stars are found in pairs. Called binary (BY-ner-ee: having two parts) stars, they revolve around each other, attracted by the other's gravitational pull. Binary stars gave scientists their first clues about black holes when they found a star that danced around an invisible partner.

Check It Out!

Black holes are invisible because the force of gravity related to them is so great, not even light can escape. To see gravity at work, go outside with a small ball. Throw it as high in the air as you can. What happens to it? This simple activity shows you how a ball thrown into the air doesn't have enough speed to escape the pull of the earth. If it did, it wouldn't fall back into your hands! For the same reason, light can't escape a black hole.

DIG DEEPER!
* black holes
* stars
* universe
* gravity

We've all heard the saying "What goes up must come down." We've also experienced it firsthand. Baseballs smacked into the outfield always curve to the ground—or a rival's mitt. A dropped glass plunges to the floor and shatters. We feel the pain of skidding across asphalt when we crash our bikes. The force that draws everything to the earth is gravity.

We may not like some of the effects of gravity, but it's a force that's helpful to us, too. Gravity keeps food from drifting off our plates. It stops us from floating away from the earth and holds the planets in orbit around the sun. Gravity even shapes distant galaxies.

physicist: (FIZZ-ih-sist) a scientist who studies matter, light, energy, sound, heat, and electricity

To discover more about electromagnetism, turn to "Invisible Energy" on page 16 and "Partners" on page 45.

As one of four forces that **physicists** have discovered at work in our universe, gravity is the least understood. We know it's a force that draws objects toward each other. The sun's pull on the earth shows us that gravity affects objects over long distances. We also know that objects with more mass—the amount of matter they're made of—have a stronger pull than objects with less mass. That's why the earth has a much greater effect on humans than humans have on one another.

> Before anything was created, He was already there. He holds everything together.
>
> COLOSSIANS 1:17

Gravity is also the weakest of the four forces. It's much weaker than electromagnetism, another force at work in our universe. Electromagnetism is responsible for light, electricity, and the combining of atoms into molecules. But it also tames electrons.

Do you remember electrons, the tiny particles that whirl around outside the atom's center, or nucleus? Do you remember that the nucleus is made of protons and neutrons? What keeps electrons from straying away from the nucleus? Electrons have a negative electric charge, while protons have a positive charge. Negative charges are drawn to positive charges. The positive charge of protons grouped within the nucleus attracts electrons, holding them in place.

The same force that draws electrons toward the nucleus also causes these tiny particles to keep their distance from each other. Negative charges push other negative charges away. Since electrons all have negative charges, they repel each other as they move about in the space of an atom.

If the negative charges of electrons push them apart, then what keeps positively charged protons from repelling each other? What keeps them from exploding out of the tightly packed nucleus? A force called the strong nuclear force works to bind protons together. This force is only at work at very close distances inside the nucleus.

Another force at work inside the nucleus is called the weak nuclear force. Like the strong nuclear force, it's found only within the nucleus. But it isn't involved in attracting objects to one another. The weak force has to do with the change—or decay—of some neutrons into protons and other particles. Atoms that change in this way are **radioactive**.

Radioactive:
(RAY-Dee-oH-AK-tiv)

A well-known physicist, Albert Einstein, believed that all four forces are part of one main force of the universe. He spent much of his life trying to figure out how they're tied together. Today, scientists continue to search for this secret.

Perhaps someday scientists will discover the key to this mystery. Even if they do, they will still have to go one step further, because there's one force even more basic. That force is God. He created everything, from atoms to galaxies. He's the One who holds everything together—

Including our lives. Sometimes it doesn't seem that way, though. Sometimes everything seems to go wrong at the same time. Our lives feel as if they're falling apart. We can feel helpless, out of control, overwhelmed. At those times we may wonder if God has forgotten about us. We may wonder if he's really in our lives.

It's not unusual to feel this way. But the next time you do, remember—

If God can hold everything together—everything from atoms to galaxies—then it's no stretch for Him to hold the details of our lives together, too. Jesus isn't like the impersonal forces that physicists study. He's interested in each of us and has our best interests at heart. He knows all about what's going on. If we stop trying to hold our own lives together and trust Him to do it for us, we can relax and find peace for our struggling hearts.

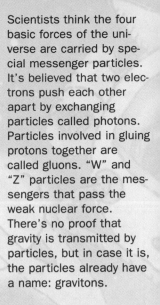

Scientists think the four basic forces of the universe are carried by special messenger particles. It's believed that two electrons push each other apart by exchanging particles called photons. Particles involved in gluing protons together are called gluons. "W" and "Z" particles are the messengers that pass the weak nuclear force. There's no proof that gravity is transmitted by particles, but in case it is, the particles already have a name: gravitons.

Match It!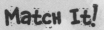

Match the force with the objects they affect.

	attracts protons and electrons
	neutrons
gravity	
	attracts two or more protons
electromagnetic force	
	keeps the earth in orbit around the sun
strong nuclear force	
	repels two or more electrons
weak nuclear force	
	repels protons from each other
	holds you to the earth

The answers are on page 152.

DIG DEEPER!

* physics
* atom
* gravity
* electromagnetism
* matter

Thought to remember:

I can relax and trust God to hold my life together.

Additional verses:

Psalm 54:4; 139:5, 17–18; Jeremiah 29:11;
Matthew 11:28; Romans 11:33–36; Hebrews 1:3

Are you a person who is curious about the unknown, who delights to explore new places or know why things work the way they do? The same curiosity sparks humans to reach into space.

In the early 1600s astronomers began to explore space with telescopes. These instruments collect light from faraway objects, focusing it so our eyes can see the objects. In the centuries that followed, bigger and better telescopes were built. But there was a problem. A blanket of air surrounds the earth. While our atmosphere allows us to breathe and protects us from harmful rays from space, it gets in the way of astronomers trying to explore the heavens. The atmosphere bends visible light traveling through it. It limits our quest for clues about space by filtering out those harmful rays. Astronomers knew they'd get a much better view if they could only get rid of the atmosphere's interference. How could they do that? Why not send a telescope *above* the atmosphere?

To discover more about the atmosphere, turn to "Inside, Outside, All Around," on page 69.

The Hubble Space Telescope is named after Edwin Hubble, an important astronomer of the 1900s.

Work on the Hubble Space Telescope, called HST or Hubble for short, began in 1977. Thirteen years later—on April 24, 1990—this forty-three-and-a-half-foot-long, 25,000-pound telescope was launched into space aboard the space shuttle *Discovery*. While orbiting 375 miles above earth, light would enter HST's tube, then bounce off a nearly eight-foot mirror onto a smaller mirror that would then aim the light into a special camera. Images recorded by the camera would be sent to computers on earth for study. Other wavelengths, from infrared to ultraviolet, could also be picked up.

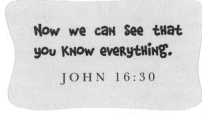

Now we can see that you know everything.

JOHN 16:30

At first the HST sent disappointing, fuzzy pictures back to earth. Its designers at NASA—National Aeronautics and Space Administration—were horrified to realize there was a tiny, tiny flaw in the eight-foot mirror. In late 1993 NASA sent another crew into space to fit the telescope with a set of mirrors and correct the flaw.

Since then Hubble has revealed new clues about planets, black holes, star-forming **nebulae**, the unbelievable numbers of stars and galaxies, and the size of our universe. The pictures it sends back are more dazzling than we could ever have imagined.

While Hubble has been sending clues to earth, astronomers have also figured out other ways to deal with the atmosphere. Some telescopes perched on the tops of moun-

nebulae: (NEH-byu-Lie) plural of "nebula"; clouds of gas and dust in space

While people train their eyes on the skies, they also search for answers inside the universe of the atom. Today, much of this work is done in particle **accelerators** (ek-SELL-uh-rate-urz). These huge instruments force beams of protons or electrons to accelerate—or speed up—until they travel at close to the speed of light. The particles then smash into targets or into beams of particles traveling in the opposite direction. Detectors record the subatomic particles that break apart or form as a result of these collisions.

Explore It!

You can explore the heavens. If there's an **observatory** (ob-ZER-vuh-tore-ee: a place with a large telescope) nearby, make plans with your family to visit. But if there isn't one, even a pair of binoculars can increase your vision of the skies. On a clear night train these "eyes" on the skies to see planets, stars, and the moon.

DIG DEEPER!

* Hubble Space Telescope
* telescope
* astronomy

tains now have computers that measure the wrinkles caused by our atmosphere and cancel them out. Some of these telescopes, with twenty-seven- to thirty-three-foot-wide mirrors, are giants that dwarf the HST. Mirrors this big can easily collect a lot of light from stars to figure out what they're made of, how fast they're spinning, their direction of movement, and distance from earth. Now instead of one space telescope, we have many eyes on the skies collecting clues.

Hubble is still important, though. It picks up ultraviolet and infrared rays that can't make it through our atmosphere. Plus, the HST still takes the clearest pictures using visible light. Plans for a larger space telescope are in the works. And on ground? Telescope creators are dreaming of mega telescopes with 100- to 330-foot-wide mirrors.

As astronomers reach into space with bigger and better instruments, some ideas about the universe are challenged, some are proven true. But there seem to be as many new questions as there are newly discovered stars and galaxies. The more we know about our universe, the more we realize how little we know about it.

Whatever way we find to peer into the heavens, one thing comes into focus: how great its Creator, God, is! He knows the answers to every question we ask—exactly how many galaxies there are, how many stars are in each galaxy, how they're born. That's no surprise—He hung each star in place and knows the name of every one. How does God know all this? God knows everything—including everything there is to know about you.

He knows the exact number of hairs on your head. He knows your thoughts and feelings, and what you're going to say before the words come out of your mouth. He knows when you sit and when you get up. He sees your every step.

If God knows us through and through, it means He also knows our deepest secrets, even the "dark" secrets we don't want anyone else to know about. But we can take comfort. Jesus also knew every one of those secrets when He took care of them for us on the cross. Our God is merciful and loving. In spite of our weaknesses and failures, He still welcomes us to know—and to be known by—Him.

Thought to remember:
God knows everything. Everything!

Additional verses:
Psalm 33:13–15; 139:1–4, 6; 147:4–5; Isaiah 40:12–14; Matthew 10:29–31; Hebrews 4:13; 1 John 3:19–20 (NIV)

60 In the Beginning

The world we live in overflows with surprises. You can find sunrises in seashells, or hear the earth sigh during gentle spring rains. You can catch the scent of love in the petals of roses, or find comfort in a patch of sunshine on frosty fall mornings. You can taste snowflake-flavored air on wintry days, or watch purple night skies blossom with stars.

If we stop to look and listen, to feel, taste, and touch, our hearts can be stirred with wonder. Our hearts can also be stirred *to* wonder: Where did all this come from?

There are different ideas about where our universe came from. We know from the very first chapter of Genesis, the first book in the Bible, that God created our universe. Not only did He create the earth—our place in space—but He also created everything else in our universe, from stars to water to man.

Many scientists believe that our earth—and the entire universe—formed as a result of an explosion of matter, called the big bang. Those who believe this **theory** think that before the explosion, all matter was compacted into a tiny, tiny space. Then, in an unbelievably hot flash, the universe began to expand. Particles that make up electrons, protons, and neutrons developed. These eventually became the elements out of which silvery stars and our blue planet took shape.

One clue that supports this idea of the big bang has to do with light. Do you remember how sunlight can be separated into the colors of the rainbow? Scientists study stars and other space objects by separating their light into the colors of the rainbow. Certain dark lines form within these rainbows because the atoms that make up objects absorb certain colors. Scientists have discovered that the dark lines from distant space objects move—or shift—toward red wavelengths of light. This is called *red shift*. It shows that stars and galaxies are moving away from the earth. To the scientists who believe in the big bang theory, the red shift shows that our universe is still expanding from an explosion that began many years ago.

theory:
(THEE-uh-ree)
an idea about why
something
happened, based
on experiments
and observations

To discover more
about how light
separates into
the colors of the
rainbow, turn to
"Rainbow of
Promises" on
page 27.

> In the beginning, God created the heavens and the earth.
>
> GENESIS 1:1
>
> He will be the sure foundation for your times, a rich store of salvation and wisdom and knowledge.
>
> ISAIAH 33:6a (NIV)

Light waves show a red shift as they move away from the earth; light waves shift toward blue wavelengths as they move toward the earth. Sound waves behave in a similar way. When an ambulance speeds toward you, the siren sounds high-pitched. As the ambulance speeds away from you, the siren sounds lower. This is called the **Doppler** (DOPP-ler) effect.

TRY It!

You can show the expansion of the universe with a balloon and a marker. First mark two dark spots on a balloon. Next, blow air into the balloon. What happens to the spots as the balloon swells? They move apart from each other! You can picture the galaxies in an expanding universe spreading apart in the same way.

DIG DEEPER!

* big bang theory
* astronomy
* red shift
* universe

We may never know for sure whether God used a big bang to begin our universe. But one thing we do know is this: If there was a big bang, it points us back to God as the creator of our universe. Why?

First, the big bang had to take place at a certain point in time; our universe had a beginning, just as we read about in Genesis. Second, the big bang leads us to ask, "Where did all the matter for such a huge explosion come from in the first place?" It couldn't have just suddenly appeared from out of nowhere. To answer this question we also have to turn to God. He's the true foundation of our universe, whether He used a huge explosion or not. God breathed the words that created the matter our universe is formed from. He marks the beginning of our universe.

Since God is the foundation of the universe, He is also the foundation of our lives. His influence goes beyond the stars, our sun, and the earth, beyond our physical bodies, all the way to our hearts. Because we owe our very beginning to God, we can also turn to Him anytime—during happy times, sad times, easy times, and hard times—and with every part of our lives. Since God is the foundation of all matter in the universe, we can trust Him with all that matters in our lives.

Thought to remember:

Since God is the foundation of all matter in the universe, I can trust Him with all that matters in my life.

Additional verses:

Job 38:4–7; Psalm 104:5; Romans 11:36 (NIV); Philippians 4:12–13 (NIV); Hebrews 11:3

Acknowledgments

T here's no doubt about it. Life is possible on earth—our place in space—because a lot of puzzle pieces work together. The same goes for the life of this book. Without the help of family, friends, and advisors, *Our Place in Space* wouldn't exist.

Steve, Josh, and Dan—I'm grateful for you. You make every day an aurora borealis day.

Karen Daniel—thanks for critiquing this manuscript, and for your friendship, too.

Phil Gronseth, Pat Blackburn, Carol March, and Dennis Wagner—what would I have done without your valuable critique of the science material in *Our Place in Space*? I learned a lot from your suggestions. Thanks also for digging up resources for me.

Russ Wiley, Judy Chilsen, John Moretti, and Mark Bennett—I appreciate the time you took to answer questions and double-check facts.

Rochelle Glöege, senior editor at Bethany House Publishers—thanks for making *Our Place in Space* possible.

Natasha Sperling, editor at Bethany House Publishers—whew! I admire your patience and endurance. You make teamwork easy.

Teri Dailey and Pam Sheldon—last, but certainly not least. Do you know what it means to me to be able to call and ask you to pray when I'm stuck? I appreciate you!

nswer Key

Answers to **FIND IT!**

in **Chapter 1,**

"Atoms, Atoms, Everywhere":

Substances made up of only one kind of atom are called **elements** (EL-uh-ments). Below is a list of elements common in our lives. Find their names in the puzzle below. Names can be found forward, backward, up, down, and diagonally.

ALUMINUM	HYDROGEN	OXYGEN
ARGON	IODINE	PLATINUM
BORON	IRON	SILVER
CALCIUM	LEAD	SODIUM
CARBON	MERCURY	SULFUR
CHLORINE	NEON	TIN
COPPER	NICKEL	TITANIUM
GOLD	NITROGEN	ZINC
HELIUM		

```
B P L E M G O L D O C D A E L Z
P N V R U I A D N N F T X N E Y
L L D E M R R X I O D I N E B R
A T N M E E W Z T K O L Q P I U
T Y E O P R T E R D N O B R A C
I B G P W M Y V O N T D O S E R
N E O N E U G I G F A N R C L E
U C R V S I L V E R Y E O M G M
M H D W P C L M N U C P N U U O
S R Y F Q L B X T H Z K J I J X
P R H U R A E H L L C Z D N B Y
X U B E W C K O C E J O I A P G
L F S C L I R W A K S H R T M E
Y L R Z N X V L W C A G Z I E N
S U H B N V U J T I O K E T X Q
T S I E W A M M U N I M U L A L
```

Answers to **MAKE IT!**

in **Chapter 19,**

"Pocket Power":

Is a lemon battery a wet- or dry-cell battery?
A wet-cell battery.

Why?
The electrolyte—lemon juice—is a liquid.

Answers to **EXPLORE IT!**

in **Chapter 21,**

"The Big Mix-Up":

Below is a list of mixtures. If you think the substance is a heterogeneous mixture, put a 1 next to it. If you think the substance is a homogeneous mixture, write a 2 next to it.

air: 2

smoggy air: 1

sandstone: 1

soil: 1

food coloring dissolved in water: 2

salt water: 2

window glass: 2

house paint: 1

water with ice cubes: 1

sand: 1

coffee: 2

a brick: 1

concrete: 1

wood: 1

Answers to Find It! in Chapter 44, "Our Place in Space":

When we believe in Jesus, He supplies us with everything we need for our lives. He provides it with His life. Here is a short list of what becomes yours when you find your place in Jesus. Find the words in the puzzle below. Words are forward, backward, up, down, and diagonal.

DIRECTION	JOY	POWER
FREEDOM	LIFE	SELF-CONTROL
GENTLENESS	LOVE	STRENGTH
GRACE	PATIENCE	TRUTH
HOPE	PEACE	WISDOM

```
Z E L P N G E N T L E N E S S F
G W A T R O M H V E X C D E B G
F H T G N E R T S R N E C L D E
I O L E N V E U S E T P H F N C
F P I P O W E R I L L T U C J B
J E O S I R B T A R D A I O L S
P A H S T M A E L D N T R N I L
K L D A C P R N Y Z C Q I T C N
R O M I E E N D Y Q I S E R N P
M V M G R A C E F I L B E O Y M
X E Y P I C S R L F M D I L G U
W T A R D E E Y M L O V L J B
H B E U L E H A W F R R S C Y K
E D X P D K H Y R M F A I R T S
T Q J O Y Z V L E L A R I P Z E
K J M H E X R S A O D L W M U R
```

Answers to Find It! in Chapter 48, "It's About Time":

The International Date Line is jagged so that it goes around countries, not through them. If this line went straight through a country, one part of a country could be a whole day ahead of another part!

Answers to Figure It! in Chapter 49, "Unsolved Mysteries":

Figure out how much you would weigh on other planets. If you weighed sixty pounds on earth, how much would you weigh on other planets? Multiply each number below by sixty (or your own weight) to find out.

Mercury: .38 X 60 = 22.8

Venus: .90 X 60 = 54

Mars: .38 X 60 = 22.8

Jupiter: 2.54 X 60 = 152.4

Saturn: 1.07 X 60 = 64.2

Uranus: .92 X 60 = 55.2

Neptune: 1.19 X 60 = 71.4

Pluto: .06 X 60 = 3.6

Answers to Explore It!
in Chapter 52, "Sun Life":

Unscramble these words to reveal the ways that the sun affects the earth.

i g l t h	light
o d o f	food
d w n i	wind
u s l d c o	clouds
r i a	air
e f l u	fuel
t t e e i i y l c c r	electricity
m t r a w h	warmth
f i l e	life

Answers to Match It!
in Chapter 54, "Which World?":

Match each description below with the right planet.

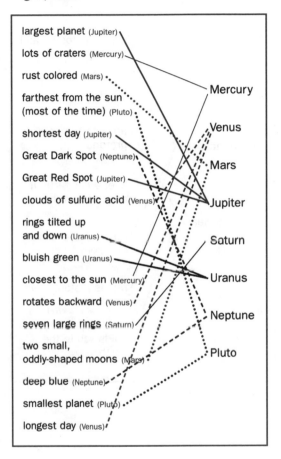

largest planet (Jupiter)

lots of craters (Mercury)

rust colored (Mars)

farthest from the sun (most of the time) (Pluto)

shortest day (Jupiter)

Great Dark Spot (Neptune)

Great Red Spot (Jupiter)

clouds of sulfuric acid (Venus)

rings tilted up and down (Uranus)

bluish green (Uranus)

closest to the sun (Mercury)

rotates backward (Venus)

seven large rings (Saturn)

two small, oddly-shaped moons (Mars)

deep blue (Neptune)

smallest planet (Pluto)

longest day (Venus)

Mercury

Venus

Mars

Jupiter

Saturn

Uranus

Neptune

Pluto

Match the force with the objects they affect.

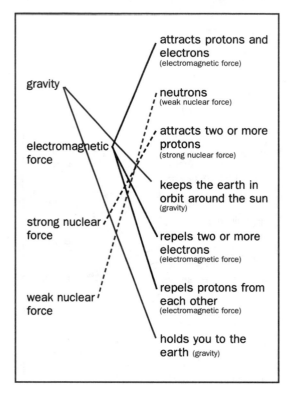

gravity

electromagnetic force

strong nuclear force

weak nuclear force

attracts protons and electrons
(electromagnetic force)

neutrons
(weak nuclear force)

attracts two or more protons
(strong nuclear force)

keeps the earth in orbit around the sun
(gravity)

repels two or more electrons
(electromagnetic force)

repels protons from each other
(electromagnetic force)

holds you to the earth (gravity)

BETHANY BACKYARD®

PICTURE BOOKS

Annie Ashcraft Looks Into the Dark
    by Ruth Senter
Annika's Secret Wish by Beverly Lewis
Cows in the House by Beverly Lewis
Fifteen Flamingos
    by Elspeth Campbell Murphy
Hold the Boat! by Jeremiah Gamble
Making Memories by Janette Oke

Princess Bella and the Red Velvet Hat
    by T. Davis Bunn
Sanji's Seed by B. J. Reinhard
Spunky's First Christmas by Janette Oke
Spunky's Camping Adventure
    by Janette Oke
Spunky's Circus Adventure by Janette Oke
What Does Love Look Like? by Janette Oke

SERIES FOR BEGINNING READERS

YOUNG COUSINS MYSTERIES by Elspeth Campbell Murphy

FIRST CHAPTER BOOK SERIES

ASTROKIDS by Robert Elmer
BACKPACK MYSTERIES
    by Mary Carpenter Reid
THE ADVENTURES OF CALLIE ANN
    by Shannon Mason Leppard

JANETTE OKE'S ANIMAL FRIENDS
    by Janette Oke
THREE COUSINS DETECTIVE CLUB®
    by Elspeth Campbell Murphy
THE CUL-DE-SAC KIDS by Beverly Lewis

NONFICTION

The Book of Jesus for Families
    by Calvin Miller
FOR ME! BOOKS by Christine Tangvald
    Board books
    Rebus books
Fins, Feathers, and Faith
    by William L. Coleman
HERO TALES: *Volumes I–IV*
    by Dave and Neta Jackson
The Wonderful Way Babies Are Made
    by Larry Christenson

Happy Easter, God!
    by Elspeth Campbell Murphy
Look What You Made, God!
    by Elspeth Campbell Murphy
*Glow-in-the-Dark Fish and 59 More Ways to
    See God Through His Creation*
    by B. J. Reinhard
*Our Place in Space and 59 More Ways to
    See God Through His Creation*
    by B. J. Reinhard

TRUSTWORTHY TALES FOR EARLY READERS

One of the key questions on parents' minds these days is whether they have to worry about the content of their early readers' books. With JANETTE OKE'S ANIMAL FRIENDS, those worries disappear. These are titles suitable for all young children and teach valuable lessons in a fun, safe way.

Colorful and featuring charming illustrations, each title features a precocious animal who uncovers important instruction on growing up—whether learning the value of family, the reasons to obey, or the importance of being yourself. The easy-to-read chapters also make the books invaluable tools for teaching little ones to read.

Spunky's Diary • *The Prodigal Cat* • *The Impatient Turtle*
This Little Pig • *New Kid in Town* • *Ducktails* • *Prairie Dog Town*
Trouble in a Fur Coat • *Maury Had a Little Lamb* • *A Cote of Many Colors*
Pordy's Prickly Problem • *Who's New at the Zoo?*

Family Treasuries of
TRUE STORIES
From the Lives of
CHRISTIAN HEROES

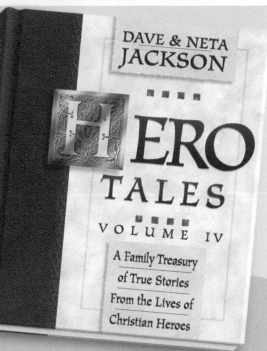

DAVE & NETA JACKSON

HERO TALES
VOLUME IV

A Family Treasury of True Stories From the Lives of Christian Heroes

Drawn from the lives of fifteen key Christian heroes, each *Hero Tales* book is a beautifully illustrated collection of exciting and educational readings. The readings are designed to inspire Christian character qualities in families with elementary-age children, and whether read together during family devotions or alone, *Hero Tales* help acquaint young readers with our heritage of Christian heroes.

HERO TALES: VOLUME I
Tales include: Amy Carmichael, Harriet Tubman, Samuel Morris, Martin Luther, Dwight L. Moody, John Wesley, and more!

HERO TALES: VOLUME II
Biographies include: Corrie ten Boom, John Bunyan, Watchman Nee, John Newton, Florence Nightingale, Jim Elliot, and others!

HERO TALES: VOLUME III
Heroes include: Billy Graham, Mother Teresa, Brother Andrew, Luis Palau, Lottie Moon, Jonathan & Rosalind Goforth, and nine more.

HERO TALES: VOLUME IV
True stories about: C.S. Lewis, Joy Ridderhof, William J. Seymour, Ricky & Sherialyn Byrdsong, John & Betty Stam, William Wilberforce, and more!

BETHANY HOUSE   11400 Hampshire Ave.S. • Minneapolis, MN 55438 • www.bethanyhouse.com • 1-800-328-6109